T5-CUU-962

The Defense Matrix

National preparedness and the military-industrial complex

by General James P. Mullins

Library of Congress Cataloging-in-Publication Data

Mullins, James P.
The defense matrix.

1. United States – Defenses. 2. Munitions – United States. I. Title.
UA23.M865 1986 355′.0213′0973 86-674
ISBN 0-932238-39-4

Avant Books®
Slawson Communications, Inc.
3719 Sixth Avenue
San Diego, CA 92103-4316

Cover design by Lillian Elaine Svec
Interior design by Mike Kelly, The Word Shop, San Diego
Editorial coordination by Nicole Mindel, Avant Books

Printed in the U.S.A.

10 9 8 7 6 5 4 3 2 1

To Barbara,
Kathryn, Karin, Lynn, Jay, and Jack

Contents

Preface

This book was written solely to help put in perspective some of the more critical national security issues of our time. Admittedly, it is biased, since it reflects my own experiences in a wide range of assignments over 38 years in uniform.

Nine of those years were spent in the Operational Requirements and Development Plans arena – first at Strategic Air Command (SAC) Headquarters during the early McNamara era and then on the Air Staff in the Pentagon when such programs as the B-1 and MX were emerging. During that period, *systems analysis* was also born, and such highly touted programs as the Skybolt, Manned Orbiting Laboratory, and the B-70, just to name a few, were dropped. By the end of that decade *total package procurement* was on its way out, and *fly-before-buy* was in. Those were also the Vietnam and Watergate years.

Then, from the vantage point of key logistics command and staff assignments and a three-year tour as Commander of SAC's Fifteenth Air Force, I witnessed the defense debacle of the 1970s – and as Commander of Air Force Logistics Command, the rush to rearm America under the Reagan Administration. In this latter position, which I held from the summer of 1981 until the fall of 1984, I was in overall charge of the logistics preparedness of all U.S. Air Force active and reserve forces worldwide, as well as logistics support to the air forces of countries receiving military assistance from the United States.

Throughout this period, defense issues have become increasingly complicated, and more and more Americans seem to be ignoring the lessons of the past in dealing with threats to our way of life. The public is confused, and the country's leaders are groping for ways to deal with real and imagined national defense problems. This uncertainty was highlighted by an October 16, 1985 Staff Report to the United States Senate Committee on Armed Services, titled *Defense Organization: The Need for Change*. It charged that the Department of Defense, to the detriment of our war fighting capabilities, had focused excessively on functional efficiency and not on the objectives and strategy of major missions.

Intended to put into perspective some of the defense issues currently being debated, this book outlines a mechanism for managing the necessary functions of manpower, research and development, and installations and logistics by the bottom line of mission capability. It does not deal with grand strategy or the conduct of war itself. Rather, it is concerned with the fundamentals of national security and specifically with the challenge of providing that security in a free society.

There is an ongoing struggle in America – and throughout the free world – between those who ignore the lessons of history and those who believe, as did the great Chinese philosopher, Sun Tzu Wu, that we must

> rely not on the likelihood of the enemy not coming,
> but on our own readiness to receive him;
> not on the chance of his not attacking,
> but rather on the fact that we have made our position unassailable.

It is tragic that, over the ages, the citizens of so many democracies have failed to heed these words, that time and again they have either neglected to provide adequate military capability or lacked the will to use it.

It would be the greatest tragedy of all time if we failed to heed Sun Tzu's words today. For more than ever before, they are the key to democracy's survival. And the United States alone has the talent and resources to make democracy unassailable.

If we are to discharge our responsibilities as citizens of our democracy and of the free world, we must understand the fundamentals of preparedness and the mechanism whereby preparedness is provided. It is my earnest hope that this book will contribute to such an understanding.

James P. Mullins
General, USAF (Ret.)

Acknowledgments

This book would not have been possible without the suggestions of many friends and associates. I am deeply indebted to each of them, especially those in the Department of Defense and the defense industry, at whose urging this book has been written. They have witnessed the events of the past few years and realize that the time is now right for change.

As for the work itself, I shall be forever grateful to those whose expertise in a wide range of disciplines was so valuable in developing the main arguments presented in the book, particularly my most able assistant and friend, Lt. Col. Leo Finkelstein, Jr.

I am also indebted to Rebecca Smith, whose editing of the manuscript made the essential points more understandable.

Finally, I am grateful to all the people in and out of uniform who have supported the ideas expressed herein, especially the men and women of the Air Force Logistics Command and the Strategic Air Command, who helped me refine and implement the concept of managing resources with combat capability as the bottom line. It is to them and people serving the cause of freedom everywhere that this book is truly dedicated.

CHAPTER 1

The Responsibilities of Citizenship

Democracy is a unique form of government, because a democracy's citizens must bear responsibilities the citizens of other forms of government do not normally have to bear. In any democracy, citizens must accept three clear-cut dimensions of responsibility: economic, political, and military. Ultimately, they decide economic policy, make political decisions, and employ military force. Those who bear the mantle of power do so only at the pleasure of the citizens, and only to do their bidding. In other forms of government, however, the functions of the state are frequently off-limits. Citizens are given no authority and consequently, have to bear little or none of the responsibility.

Economics and Politics

The majority of American citizens readily accept their economic responsibilities: they learn skills, find employment, earn money, buy goods and services, and make investments. In fact, a great deal of emphasis is placed by our society on impressing its citizens, through both formal and informal means, of their obligations in this regard. Americans spend much time and effort learning the economic ropes. There's a great deal of information available on everything from money market rates to home mortgage options, from stock market prices to tax shelters.

Most citizens also accept their political responsibilities,

although sometimes not so readily. Variations in voting behavior attest to this. But we still teach civics in high schools, and many disciplines require courses in federal, state, and local government at the college level. Plus a great deal of media attention is always focused on the functioning of government, particularly at election time, when the need for information is greatest – and especially during presidential elections, when numerous tutorials flood the news stands and airwaves with information on such things as how the delegate system works, what the Electoral College does, how campaigns are waged, and what the various opinion polls show.

The Abrogation of Military Responsibility

For many Americans, however, the third dimension of responsibility – that of defending the country – is somehow abrogated to other people "who do that kind of thing." Americans tend to reject any personal involvement in the defense effort. They shy away from learning how the military functions, or what this nation's defense posture is, or by what means it's even developed. And in particular, they're ignorant of how the military relates to the other two legs of our society – the economic and political legs.

For many Americans, military concerns serve as a distraction from other, more important dimensions of civic responsibilities. And that's a great irony – because no dimension of responsibility is more important than the protection of those freedoms that allow us to be what we are, that allow our free enterprise economy to grow, and that allow our democratic political system to function.

The military function, of course, is often viewed as the least pleasant part of our society. After all, it's more fun to make money than to get shot at – and it's more acceptable to achieve one's goals through political influence than brute force. For most Americans, the military is identified with pain and conflict, death and suffering, and great destructive power.

Perhaps that's why, as we've seen in so many democracies through the ages, the requirement for a strong military force and the resources necessary to meet this requirement are often rejected out of hand, at least to some degree. And so is any opportunity to learn more about what a reliable defense requires in terms of resources, to understand how the defense process works, and to become personally involved in that process.

In our society, especially since the end of World War II when over 15 million civilians wore the uniform, individual citizens have been drifting away from defense concerns. More and more, they've become isolated from what the American military is all about – and they've been cut off from facts about how we actually provide for our security.

That's not to say, of course, that they've drifted away from the economic or political implications of defense issues. Today there's plenty of concern with such things as waste in the military-industrial complex, bloated defense budgets, and spare parts over-pricing. And frankly, much of this concern is justified. The economic and political implications of these shortcomings are bad enough – but more than that, they also indicate lessened defense capability, which is the purpose for the American military in the first place.

Like all large bureaucracies, the military-industrial complex does have its share of problems. It is particularly prone to focusing on internal, organizational interests often to the detriment of the output the organization is designed to produce. In other words, its structure and operation have often evolved without enough regard to its function.

Criticism of the military-industrial complex is not bad in and of itself. If it produces good, creative solutions that improve the operation of the organization, the criticism can be invaluable. More often, however, such criticism is either off-target, failing to address the real crux of defense problems, or it's based on an inadequate understanding of the military, thus yielding no useful solutions.

Americans really don't appreciate the military-industrial complex for what it is. They don't understand how it works, why we need it, or what its problems really are. They don't view defense issues in the same way they view economic policy and political movements. It's no wonder that there's been a great misunderstanding of such defense issues as spare parts pricing.

Part of the problem is that our citizens are becoming

increasingly cutoff from the harsh realities of today's international environment – realities that call for the existence of a strong military capability. And the opportunities for them to study and understand the often difficult and painful sacrifices required if these realities are to be dealt with effectively are steadily decreasing.

Why are they so unaware of defense matters? It's been four decades since the last world war – four decades since 15 million American citizen-soldiers experienced the brutality and inhumanity that characterizes much of the world today. Yet even then, they experienced it not in their homeland, but across far-away foreign shores. For many Americans today, the savagery of Pearl Harbor, or the nightmare of the Holocaust is, at most, a faint memory of something read in a history book or seen on a television miniseries.

Many Americans fail to even recognize the price of being free, much less be willing to pay the price. They seem openly hostile to the government, especially to that part of it responsible for fighting the nation's wars. They support, often with their silence, those far more deserving of condemnation. And they see little connection between maintaining a strong military capability and maintaining their economically and politically secure society.

A generation is now in the process of inheriting the leadership, and consequently, the defense of this nation. They have never really been threatened, and in many cases do not appreciate the military capabilities that survival demands. Some even live in a make-believe world, oblivious to the danger that grows around them. Their ignorance of the need for a strong defense, or the requirements inherent in maintaining the requisite military capability, renders them incapable of protecting a democracy.

A Return to Concerns of the Past

In the past, whenever war came, our nation has had time to respond adequately to the threat. In the process, our citizens have been able to acquire, often through personal experience, an appreciation of what the military is all about. But given the power of modern technology, a fighting war could come too fast for either the wherewithal or proper attitudes to develop.

In the early years of our country, defense concerns were as great, if not greater, than economic or political issues – because survival was clearly on the line then. The frontier settlers had to be ready to fight, because they never knew when or where their vital interests would be attacked, and they never knew how much time they would have to get their act together.

Today we've come full circle. Again, we must be ready to fight, because again, we no longer know when and where our vital interests may be attacked. The power and speed of modern military technology allow no time to build and mobilize a military capability once the need arises. What this means is that, like the frontier settlers of yesteryear, we can no longer rely on having time to get our act together.

That's why today the responsibility for defending this country must be more readily accepted by more American citizens. They must understand the nature of the threat and how to go about dealing with it. They must recognize that the loss of wealth, freedom, and life are real possibilities and appreciate and fully exploit the inherent strengths our society has for defending itself – strengths that include a thirst for innovation and a free enterprise system that can turn innovation into tangible achievements.

Dealing with the Problem

Americans must also recognize the real problem facing defense today is the relationship between our resources and priorities. Our society can no longer do everything it wants to do, and we must make tough decisions about what really needs to be done first. For American citizens, that means facing up to harsh realities, breaking free of well-developed but outdated mind-sets about defense, and understanding what it takes to provide for our national security – not only in terms of resources, but also in terms of how these resources are managed and used.

This book is meant to be of some help in that regard. It's thrust is not just to identify the problems, but to offer solutions and to provide guidelines for viewing and understanding many of today's significant military issues.

We'll start off by looking at priorities and the need to get them straight. Achieving excellence is the focus, especially against the rising tide of institutionalized mediocrity, including military and industrial mediocrity. From education to arms production, we're falling further and further behind, no longer setting the standard of excellence, and in many cases, allowing the standard itself to decay. This alone portends serious problems ahead given the very competitive world environment and the requirement to achieve excellence in order to compete in that environment. And it indicates a real need in our society for leadership able to achieve excellence.

Next we'll look at the proclivity of some people to deny the unpleasant and the impact this inclination has had historically. The argument is that man has a savage aspect by nature, one that often becomes dominant when the available resources cannot totally satisfy everyone's desires. Throughout history, free societies have tended to deny this harsh reality – and the results have often been disastrous. As demand for resources increases, especially from third world nations, each nation must achieve excellence, including military excellence, or run the real risk of forfeiting its position, its wealth, and even its survival.

Our next concern will be the excellence-inhibitor of outdated mind-sets, especially outdated mind-sets in the defense business. We often accept the mediocre in defense as being good enough – and we do that, in part, because we still do things today basically like we did them during the postwar years of the '40s and '50s. This mind-set is making us less competitive at a time when we can least afford it – and in an arena where we can least afford it.

We now have a private sector defense industry set up to produce large numbers of new systems, when we no longer buy large numbers of new systems. And we now keep systems much longer (often 300 percent longer than originally designed), which establishes the requirement for much larger amounts of follow-on support such as spare parts, replacement engines, and so on. Yet our industrial base for supplying such support has not only withered from years of neglect but also is out of sync with that requirement. We will take a closer look at logistics support by relating logistics to modern life. Then our focus will shift to logistics in military terms – and why it poses so great a constraint on our national defense capability.

We'll then take an in-depth look at what happens when weapon systems are so unreliable they require a great deal of follow-on support, when the defense industrial base is not keyed to providing this support, and when this arrangement is neglected over a period of years. We'll also consider perhaps the most celebrated logistics problem: spare parts overpricing. The goal is to put the problem into perspective and to provide an overview of the causes and how they relate to one another.

Then we'll look at a new solution to the problem of providing adequate logistics support – one unencumbered by outdated mind-sets from the past. Its basic premise is that new technology can remove the burden of buying spare parts and providing elaborate, costly maintenance by simply improving the reliability of the systems themselves. Over the next 30 years, the savings in terms of dollars just from Air Force systems alone could all but retire the entire national debt. And, of course, improved reliability would substantially enhance our ability to deter aggression and defend our national security.

The military-industrial complex itself – what it historically has done for this nation, what it contributes today, and what its significant problems really are – is our next area of concern. We will consider the alternatives to our present system and the main task for the future: creating a far more integrated military-industrial complex.

Finally, a bottom-line approach to management will be proposed – a philosophy and management system that has the proven capability of allocating scarce defense resources across the board throughout the military-industrial complex with the goal of providing the best possible combat capability. Called "meaningful measures of merit," this system is designed to respond when requirements have to be met but the resources to do so are inadequate.

Designed to give Americans the information they need so that they can make informed decisions about the military-industrial complex, the pages ahead will help shed some light on what historically has been the most important responsibility of democratic citizenship: ensuring the security of the state by having an effective military capability.

CHAPTER 2

Excellence, Leadership, and Survival

In a very real way, we've now come full circle — back to those vulnerabilities that once characterized the American frontier. We're traveling down a road potted with dangers the likes of which we, as a nation, haven't traveled in over 200 years. And some very tough choices have to be made if we're to continue moving ahead.

In the coming years, as the threat to our democratic way of life increases, the resources available to meet that threat will continue falling into shorter supply — and the demand for these resources, especially among emerging nations, will continue to increase. That's why we, as a society, must now move to get our priorities straight. And of all the priorities we must address, we have to put achieving military excellence at the top of the list.

Getting Priorities Straight

We now find throughout American society a shared, social inability to get our priorities straight — to allocate national resources effectively, to make the right decision when a fork in the road appears. But that shouldn't be too surprising, since during the past two hundred years or so, making the right decision hasn't been all that important — not with the tremendous surplus of resources we controlled, the protective isolation we enjoyed, and the ingenuity we commanded.

That's why the United States is still, with little doubt, the greatest and most powerful country in the world. It still commands tremendous resources, has the most powerful economy, and still has the inherent strengths of a free society, which effectively stimulate innovation and the achievement of excellence. But very rapidly, we're approaching a crossroads in our fulfillment as a nation, a critical intersection in the life cycle of our democracy. The road ahead diverges into two paths, and the one we take will decide our future.

In his poem "The Road Not Taken," Robert Frost writes about two roads diverging in a yellow wood, one that was frequently traveled, and one that was not, one that would lead to failure, and one that would lay out a path to success. The persona of the poem, as we know, took the road less traveled — and for him, that made all the difference.

As a nation, we've often taken the other path — the one most traveled — and time and again, we've gotten away with it. But we can't continue to get away with it, not with the competition in the world as tough as it's getting, not with the political, economic, and military vulnerabilities we now have, and not with our very survival on the line.

The situation we're facing today is really nothing new. In fact, it's not unlike that which we, as a people, initially faced on the North American continent when those in the first expedition from the Old World landed at Jamestown in 1607. They too had a problem with their priorities and failed to give the realities of their environment — the harsh winters, serious disease, and hostile neighbors — due consideration.

Too few of the settlers were willing to work cultivating the fields, while too many of them preferred to search for gold and not for food, shelter, and security. What followed was the horrible starving time, the winter of 1609 when almost 90 percent of Jamestown's population perished from famine and disease.

But Jamestown was lucky — it had a second chance. The next time, the other path was taken. The next time, the colony's priorities were on target. Resources and effort were put into agricultural development, storehouses were constructed, and sufficient numbers of laborers were brought in. In effect, the new settlers and adventurers did what they had to do: keyed resource allocation directly to the basics of life, to those things necessary for survival.

Our history as a nation really began with that colony at Jamestown. And since that first terrible experience, we've usually done what we've needed to do. In those early, formative years of colonization, we concentrated our resources and efforts principally on surviving — because acquiring the food, shelter, and defense necessary to sustain life was, in and of itself, a full-time job.

As our nation matured, however, we realized just how blessed we were in both the resources and the talent to exploit them. Indeed, once we had established our democracy and built an infrastructure to guarantee our survival — to provide the food we eat, the shelter we live in, and the protection we need — we turned our attention to improving the quality of life.

And for the next 200 years, that's the road we've traveled, exploiting our resource-rich environment. We chomp away at our resources ever faster, taking larger and larger bites. Finally we became accustomed to using far more than we needed merely for sustenance alone. Of course, there were episodic throwbacks to an earlier time, the most notable of which was the Great Depression. On the whole, however, compared with what the rest of the world had to face during this same period, our requirements for survival were far less than the resources available to us.

The result today is that this nation is incredibly well off. One need only fly over any big metropolitan area — over thousands of acres of suburban homes, summer camps, and elaborate road systems — or travel throughout foreign lands to realize just how good we have it in this country.

For hundreds of years, we've enjoyed a growth curve and standard of living unprecedented in the history of humanity. For hundreds of years, we've had virtually every resource we could desire, we've had a homeland essentially unscarred by the ravages of war, and we've had the innovation and know-how to be productive and to make the system work. In fact, that has been our key to achieving excellence — and frankly, that has provided unheard of luxury for the vast majority of our citizens today.

The Need To Achieve Excellence

Achieving excellence is the life blood of any democracy — particularly our democracy. Free enterprise systems like ours rise and fall directly as a function of their productivity and accomplishment. That's why we must be very careful not to let our productivity and accomplishment wane. No longer do we live in splendid isolation from the ills that have always plagued most of humanity, no longer are we invulnerable to political, economic, and military pressures from abroad, and no longer do we command every resource and control every need. For us, the world has changed, and the competitive environment has changed: no longer are we guaranteed survival — political, economic, or military.

Our objective must be to deal effectively in a new kind of competitive environment. We still have the resources and know-how to do very well, but many other nations also have resources, the know-how, national will, and sense of purpose to compete very effectively, as well. Today, the United States is part of a community of nations all actively vying for the scarce resources necessary even for life itself. It's a tough competition, one often characterized by fierce diplomatic, economic, political, and military conflicts, where the outcome may well mean survival or extinction for some or all of the competitors.

Throughout history, many have sought an idealized balance in life, where all the world's people could work together, giving freely of themselves to create a secure and mutually supportive international community. Of course, this has never happened, and perhaps it never will. Human desire has always outrun the resources necessary to satisfy that desire. Just being alive puts us into competition. Whether we like it or not, this competition has one overriding rule: those who succeed in identifying and achieving excellence will be those who ultimately survive.

At the end of World War II, this nation was better at achieving excellence than any other country on the face of the earth. There was virtually no resource we could not control, no human endeavor we had not taken the lead in. From heavy industry to medicine, from electronic technology to military power, the United States was clearly out in front. And it was from this position that we learned to view the world. If we wanted the best car, we bought American; if we wanted the best radio, we bought American. The best movies were American made. Indeed, the best of almost everything resulted from American designs and American craftsmanship, because this country consistently pursued and achieved excellence and set the standard throughout the world.

But in recent years, Detroit has not set the standard for excellence in automotive design and production. It has forfeited much of that role to foreign shores. Nor have our consumer electronics manufacturers continued to set the standard for excellence in radio and television production. They too have allowed these functions to migrate overseas.

The evidence is mounting that many countries are now actively pursuing various forms of excellence in order to compete more effectively. Industrially, for example, we have seen Japan become one of the most highly competitive giants in the world. During the past 20 years or so, we've compromised our competitive edge in a variety of industrial endeavors, and perhaps we've even started to pay the price in terms of skills lost, jobs forfeited, and successes denied.

This trend is disturbing, because in recent years while many of the world's nations have moved to institutionalize excellence in response to the competitive challenge, we have not. According to the evidence, we've often done exactly the opposite: we've moved to institutionalize mediocrity — a direction that, in the international economic environment, has already had serious impact and could well portend even more ominous implications for our future.

Institutionalized Mediocrity

At the heart of the difficulties we face is something called *institutionalized mediocrity*: the growing American tendency to accept the average as being good enough. Such mediocrity apparently stems from our shared inability to differentiate or discriminate between clearly dissimilar alternatives where function or worth demands such distinctions be made.

Most of us, of course, do discriminate every day just to avoid pain and to stay alive. We must decide what is hot and what is cold, what is dangerous and what is safe, what is poisonous and what is edible — and we must distinguish between friends and foes, and strengths and weaknesses. But where pain or survival isn't immediately apparent, for some reason, we often shrink from making these decisions. We seemingly reward those who do not make these discriminations. Like a teacher who can't bear to give a bad grade, we effectively compress the exceptional and the not-so-exceptional, or one function and another function, into a non-threatening, bland uncertainty.

As a society, we subscribe to the notion that all people should have an equal opportunity to excel, but we often forget that excellence presupposes some type of clear differentiation between good and bad, success and failure — and that if we fail to distinguish between the two extremes, then we'll see everything as average and have no choice but to accept the mediocre as our standard.

But could it be that, in an effort to eliminate the kinds of harmful discrimination based on arbitrary indicators of race, religion, sex, or national origin, we've lost sight of the need for discrimination based on fact — the type necessary for survival? Could it be we've forgotten that equality of opportunity is equal opportunity to prove unequal talents? Arbitrary, superficial discrimination weakens society, but our actions often seem designed to make all talents appear equal, whether they are or not. In the process of trying to make everyone with unequal talents and abilities equal, we've been propping up the less capable and holding back the more capable — and in the process, artificially limiting what we are and what we can become. We have started down that road to institutionalized mediocrity, thereby endangering the very freedom of opportunity we strive to protect.

Hasn't this already begun to insidiously rob us of that competitive spirit which makes us great, reducing the chances of our finding the Edisons, Carvers, and Einsteins of tomorrow? Less and less our society is rewarding that special urge to be above average. More and more we're looking only for the image of superiority. Yet it's a superficial image we seek, one that reality may have little relevance to what we actually find.

For example, consider the all-too-typical college course in which it's no longer so important to *earn* an A or B as it is just to *get* an A or B. An A or B has become the expected in many courses at many schools; getting a C is terribly painful, getting a D is virtually unthinkable, and getting an F in many cases is almost impossible.

Of course, this wasn't so 30 or 40 years ago, when a C really did represent average, competent work, and an A was something very special. The grade inflation we've been seeing in our schools does not represent more excellence; it represents more institutional mediocrity. One need only consider that as grades have compressed at the upper end of the spectrum, national scholastic test scores over the past 20 years have shown a disturbing overall downward trend.

Grades haven't gotten better because students have gotten better. Rather, grades have gotten better because we've failed to distinguish between the exceptional and the average. And, as many admissions directors will attest to today, a transcript alone has lost much of its value in terms of predicting relative performance or future potential. Because of institutionalized mediocrity, it's becoming harder and harder to identify and truly challenge gifted students – those with the intellect and ambition we must have to compete in a world full of gifted, ambitious intellects that are being challenged and against which we will have to compete.

The problem, of course, is not unique to the academic segment of American society. Academic grades simply reflect in a visible and empirical way the debilitating mind-set that has infected our population as a whole. Throughout our society, we seem to want so much for everyone to have the chance to win that we try and *wish away* the reality of losing. In effect, we've wound up trying to make everyone a winner. Just attend a Little League awards banquet sometime where virtually everyone gets an award. Here, and about everywhere else, we seem to have lost sight of our original goal: to provide an environment where everyone has a chance to succeed, and where making oneself a success can still build a path leading to self-fulfillment and meaning in life.

We no longer seem to accept that a certain amount of pain is necessary for achievement, that without adversity, conflict, and the chance of failure, there can really be no success. If we somehow succeed in making everyone a winner, then we'll all be the losers, because success will have lost its meaning.

The trend toward institutional mediocrity is increasing, and the signs of it are all around us. Just look at business in this country today where we, as a nation, provide vast amounts of financial support for the unsuccessful, restrict by bureaucratic regulation anyone who tries to get ahead, and punish with high taxes and pay caps anyone who somehow succeeds. Then, we seem surprised when our productivity falls.

But it's not just business and productivity that are victimized. It's also the little things in our everyday lives. Certainly all of us have fallen prey to mediocrity in many small, innocuous ways because of the difficulty of discriminating. For example, what happens when you move to a new town and try to find a *good* dentist? Clearly there's a real need here to identify which dentists are good and which ones are not so good. But there's no formalized structure to really supply the evaluative information necessary to make a sound choice. The structure of the profession, like society itself, inhibits such distinctions.

Of course, given the importance of teeth in everyday life, there is a real need to discriminate. So what do we do? We usually turn to word of mouth, talk to our neighbors and friends, and based on the data we collect in this haphazard manner, we try to discriminate: we try to make a clear choice within a group where relative excellence has been lost in an abstract average.

Similar problems also exist in other areas. Just think about what we often go through to select an auto mechanic, plumber, or television repairperson before we find one competent to do a good job at a fair price. The lack of discriminants among our trades people is a clear indicator of the problem. Indeed, modern realities seem a far cry from the guilds of the past. Today, in many areas, we've changed our focus from *quality* to *seniority*. We've created a system in which there is little distinction among unequal talents, a system that often snuffs out the flame of enthusiasm and creativity in our more ambitious and capable people. The goal in life today is often not so much to excel, to stand out from the crowd, but rather to get by, to survive by fitting into the anonymity of modern mediocrity.

Military Excellence and the Future

Now what does this all mean for the future of our democracy? And what does this say about what we're doing, and what we should be doing? When you talk about survival in the '80s and beyond, what you're really talking about is our taking a serious look at how we're setting our priorities and in what direction American society is heading. There's a great need today for an honest evaluation of the excellence we're achieving – and not just in terms of some ivory tower criteria of what excellence is, but in terms of how well what we're doing really stacks up in the various arenas of international competition.

The most dangerous and dynamic area of international competition is, of course, the military arena – where an outcome can be rapidly decided by force against force, or by the mere threat of force against force. Here military excellence involves the willingness to end armed conflicts on favorable terms, and the clear capability to do so – no matter how, when, or where the conflicts may occur. Yet for some reason, achieving and discriminating the kind of excellence in this competitive area is perhaps the most controversial and difficult challenge for many Americans today.

As a civilized society, we must work for a diplomatic solution to the inevitable conflicts of life – a solution based exclusively on social, political, and economic considerations. But we must never forget, as many nations have, just why diplomacy works. We must never ignore the lessons of history on this point. For diplomacy to be an effective means of resolving conflict, it must represent to both sides the alternative with the greatest number of advantages.

Diplomacy is based on relative power – political, economic, and military – and on those alternatives that power provides each side to pursue its national goals. If the balance of military power is such as to rule out military action (a situation called *mutual deterrence*), then diplomacy is far more likely to work.

That's why, in terms of finding peaceful solutions to our economic, political, and cultural conflicts, a balance of terror is a far better thing than an imbalance of terror. And although we must clearly work to reduce the relative level of terror, we must only do so in a way that will keep our power and power of our potential adversaries in relative balance. If for no other reason, we must place our priorities on achieving military excellence because that's where our potential adversaries are placing their priorities.

Figure 1 demonstrates our reluctance to make military procurement and research and development as great a priority as the Soviets have. Figure 2 demonstrates the increasing priority our potential adversary has placed on improving military excellence.

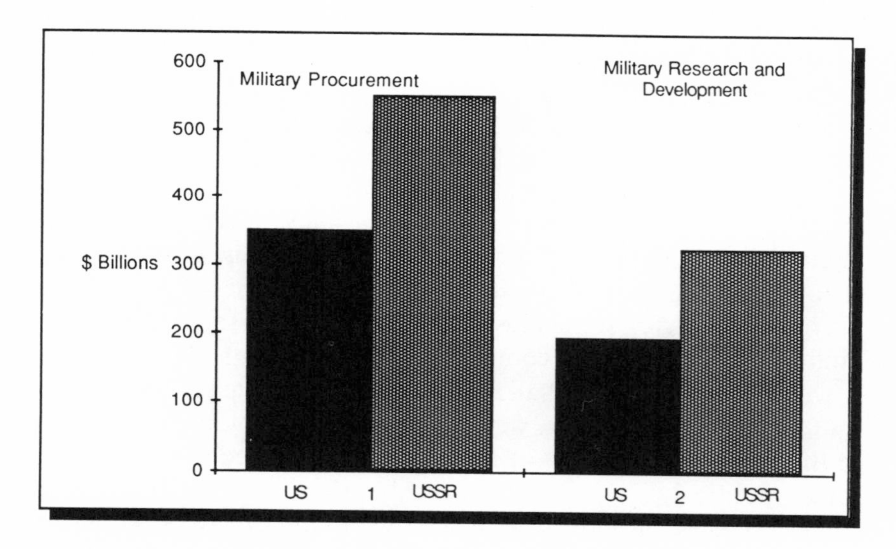

Fig. 1. Ten-Year Selected Defense Cost Comparisons. *(Data from* Soviet Military Power, *3d ed., Washington, D.C.: U.S. Government Printing Office, April 1984, p. 99.)*

Consider the Strategic Defense Initiative (SDI), the so-called Star Wars system designed to defend against ballistic missile attack. Some in our society argue that we should not militarize space, believing if we don't take advantage of space for military purposes, no one else will either. Others believe that building a ballistic missile defense would upset the current balance of power, and further escalate the arms race.

Both of these beliefs represent a clear denial of a very harsh

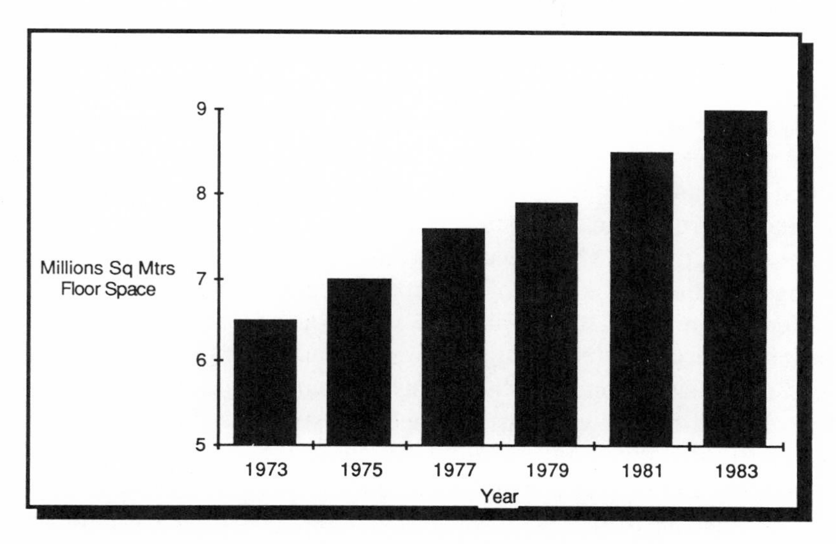

Fig. 2. Growth in Key Soviet R&D and Test Facilities.
(Data from Soviet Military Power, *3d ed., Washington, D.C.: U.S. Government Printing Office, April 1984, p. 104.)*

reality – that the Soviets are already doing what they argue so strongly against our doing. Just consider the Soviet's antisatellite program. Many Americans don't think we need such a capability, but they ignore the fact that the Soviets have, and have had for some time now, the operational capability to attack our satellites in near-earth orbit. Not only do they have a pellet-type interceptor they can launch into space, they also have ground-based, high-energy lasers with antisatellite capabilities.

This poses a serious threat, because it will soon be very difficult, if not impossible, to conduct effective military operations (that is, achieve military excellence) without the surveillance, weather, navigation, and command/control/communications capabilities provided by space assets. The day is not far away when the untimely loss of certain critical space systems in the high-tech, high-stakes military environment will be tantamount to losing a major battle in a war – or even worse.

In terms of SDI, the Soviets have been busy now for the past 25 years. For two and a half decades, they've also been moving forward in a clear and determined effort to blunt the effect of U.S. and Allied retaliation for any Soviet attack. They already have the only operational ballistic missile defense system in the world — one that protects their capital city of Moscow — and one that they've been upgrading and expanding while publicly condemning our stated desire to pursue such a defense.

Additionally, the Soviets have initiated a substantial research program into the kinds of advanced technologies necessary for defense against ballistic missiles: space-based particle beams and kinetic-energy systems, high-powered radio-frequency weapons, and specialized computer and sensor technologies.

In just these two areas — space and strategic defense — it isn't hard to imagine what would happen if we fell well behind in achieving military excellence — if, out of some misguided fear of escalating the arms race, we allowed the Soviets to unilaterally become invulnerable to the strategic retaliatory capability the free world depends on to protect it from nuclear attack.

Achieving Military Excellence

When looking at military excellence, it's important to understand that, like any excellence, it's a product of capability, effort, and momentum. For example, how many times have you seen a superior basketball team that has pulled out in front try to slow down a game or take a game for granted? And how many times has that team destroyed its own momentum, and in the end, deprived itself of the excellence it was trying to achieve? The same thing could easily happen to us in the military arena, except, in this case, we'd stand to lose far more than just a basketball game.

Clearly there's a need for Americans to achieve more excellence, especially in the military arena. But how do you get them to do what they need to do? Basically there's three ways: you can tell them to do it, you can pay them to do it, or you can inspire them to do it.

Telling them to do it doesn't work well in our kind of society.

For one thing, Americans are traditionally very independent, especially of centralized government authority. And for another, our legal system stands firmly behind this independence. Given the kinds of legal delays Americans can generate in fighting almost any government order, and given the time constraints often associated with achieving military excellence, we can't rely on legal authority alone – not in this case.

The second method of getting people to do what is necessary is paying them to do it. This works very well in our society, at least up to a certain point. The military and private industry attract, and in effect, control people by offering packages of wages and benefits. And both the military and private industry offer other inducements, such as providing people with the opportunity to learn skills and seek additional education.

But the day of the true mercenary is ending as more and more Americans draw the line as to what they will do for money alone. Indeed, you can no longer simply pay people enough to endure serious sacrifices in terms of family, careers, or even life itself. The socioeconomics of modern American society simply will not support such an approach – at least not over the long haul. The military and the defense industry can attract the best, brightest, most skilled people for a time by paying them alone, but ultimately, the cost will exceed what can be afforded.

The Alternative of Leadership

The third way to get people to do what they need to do is by inspiring them to do it – and that means leadership. In fact, the underlying prerequisite for achieving military-industrial excellence today is leadership. In a technological age, where nanoseconds and microseconds can determine profit or loss, success or failure, and even life or death, having the inspiration of real leadership becomes the paramount concern.

The danger today is that we've tended to substitute management in situations where leadership is required. And although both managers and leaders are essential for this nation's survival, they're not equal, nor are they even similar. Managers manage things, and leaders lead people. Managers work with empirical descriptions of things as they are — they're concerned with numbers, regression curves, and quantities. The work of managers can be precisely measured and described, and the result of their efforts verified.

Leaders, on the other hand, determine how things will be and how best to motivate people to do what needs to be done. They function not so much with numbers and quantities as with human nature. The work of leaders cannot be precisely described and measured, nor can the results of their efforts be verified.

In our society, we tend to measure what can be easily measured, and we tend to ignore that which cannot be easily measured. But beyond that, we also tend to ascribe importance to that which we can readily measure. For example, we often fall into the trap of ascribing more importance to such things as political polls, IQ scores, and inflation rates than they really deserve.

We rely on political polls to tell us who's going to win an election, IQ scores to tell us how intelligent a person is, and inflation rates to tell us how fast the cost of living is going up. But political polls only demonstrate, within a window of statistical error, what the attitudes of the population are in a slice of time. They don't account for longer periods of time, and they cannot guarantee that attitudes will necessarily translate into voting behavior.

IQ scores demonstrate the ability of a person to deal with abstractions on perhaps 3 or 4 dimensions of human capability, although there's good evidence that perhaps 20 or more dimensions exist. Additionally, these scores do not reflect the intelligence of the person on what few dimensions are measured, but rather, the opportunity he or she has had to learn during formative childhood years.

And finally, inflation rates cause all kinds of people to do all kinds of things and make all kinds of investments — all in the name of staying ahead. But chances are that what they're trying to stay ahead of isn't real. That's because inflation rates are based on a whole spectrum of data, including food prices, energy costs, and home ownership. But if they're not, say, buying a home, the inflation rate does not represent their true situation.

The point of all this is that we tend to make the less important *more* important when we can precisely measure it. And we tend to make the more important *less* important when we cannot precisely measure it. When this is combined with the power of new technology, the impact on leadership in our society then becomes easier to understand.

Modern technology, especially data processing and telecommunications technology, gives us great power to manipulate data. And the more power we have to do so, the more we do it. We cannot, however, manipulate data on leadership because it's just not available. We cannot precisely describe or evaluate leadership. Like predicting the winner of an upcoming election, measuring the creativity dimension of intelligence, or evaluating the loss of buying power of every American family, it just doesn't lend itself to precise description.

But that's not true for management. Our power to measure has increased — and with it, so has the relative importance we've given to the management process we're measuring. We've even come to the point today where we often treat it as a more important factor than leadership.

American society tends to reject real leaders because they rock the boat, they challenge the status quo, they keep the system in tension, they're unpredictable, and they make people feel uncomfortable. Leaders are only tolerated when technology fails, when things really go wrong, and when there's no other choice — and they're readily discarded once the need subsides.

That's why, in politics, academics, industry, and the military, we've placed management on a pedestal above leadership. One need only look at the number of staffers, campaign managers, and pollsters in American politics today, at the number of management courses in colleges and universities, at the emphasis placed on management in our factories and businesses, and at how many military and corporate officers are promoted today — not because they possess the human skills of a leader, but because they have demonstrated the technical skills of a manager.

Expanding technology has created an environment that now demands absolutely the achievement of excellence. And that means having solid leadership skills in positions of power where real decisions can be made and meaningful actions taken. That means electing political leaders to be leaders, not to be the mouthpieces for staffs of managers. That means seriously developing the concept of leadership in our colleges and universities and coming up with a better system to identify those with real leadership talent. That means hiring tough, bright, innovative people in business and industry, putting them in charge, and letting them lead the way. And, in the military, that means promoting and filling leadership positions with more leaders and less managers.

Implications for the Military – and for Everyone Else

For the American military, the implication of all this is that the free ride is over. Today's international situation demands that we be ready to defend this nation's interests against potential adversaries who are very brutal, very strong, and very bright – potential adversaries who consistently achieve a great deal of excellence in the military arena.

That means having enough well-trained and inspired people who are ready and willing to fight and having adequate numbers of capable weapon systems which are sustainable in combat. For the day may soon come when we'll be called out – and if that happens, we'd better not be bluffing. We'd better have the cards to play out the hand and win.

But what kind of cards are we holding today? Four aces, or four jokers – wild cards that may or may not be of value, depending on the particular game we have to play. Years ago, when we approached an earlier crossroads, we decided, because of economic and political realities, to compromise our standard of excellence. In effect, the military replaced its aging weapon systems at the expense of support, since it couldn't have both. It redefined excellence as having the weapon system, without regard for how well it could be sustained in combat. For example, in the case of the Air Force, priority was placed on designing systems to fly fast and high but not on doing so reliably.

To the extent the systems were not reliable, we also failed to buy enough spares and repair parts to keep them going. In addition, we permitted the defense industrial base to wither. We allowed it to be unduly criticized, and we limited its ability to modernize and prosper. We've seen competition wane, productivity fall, overseas process dependencies develop, and lead times lengthen considerably.

The result? Today we can't fully support even the peacetime mission of our weapon systems, much less sustain them in time of war. Like a student receiving A's for C work, we've been pursuing the image of combat capability – yet, in many cases the real substance of true achievement is lacking.

Years ago, perhaps following this course made more sense. After all, there was little likelihood that someone would call our hand – not with the political, economic, and military superiority we possessed, not with the defense industrial might we had at our finger tips, and not with the security we enjoyed. But today the world is full of competitive, hostile forces, any one of which could call us out at any time – and in far away but vital areas of the globe. And our ability to meet this challenge is falling into more serious question.

What this means is that those responsible for defending this nation – including political, business, and military leaders – must choose the right road to travel. They must best use the resources available to provide the kind of defense industry this nation requires, and they must formulate strategy, tactics, doctrine, and force structure that doesn't just have the appearance of military excellence, but that is, in fact, excellent.

If what we do only gives the appearance of excellence, then we need to find another way to do it. If the organization of the military-industrial complex doesn't make sense, given modern realities, then we need to reorganize. And if our processes, like planning, programming, and budgeting, aren't working for us, then we need to change them.

CHAPTER 3

The Denial of Harsh Realities

People just naturally don't like the unpleasant – and as individuals, groups, and societies, they'll go to extraordinary lengths to avoid it. That's why it's often so difficult to achieve excellence – because it can be exceptionally painful to admit excellence is not being achieved or to do what has to be done to achieve it.

But avoiding such harsh realities never makes them better. Ironically, it only makes them harsher, because as the severity of the problem gets worse and the demand on resources increases, the time available to marshal these resources and solve the problem diminishes. The ultimate result then is often fewer resources, no time, and an even more serious problem that may no longer be solvable.

Perhaps of all the harsh realities man has to face, warfare is the harshest. In fact, warfare is the single greatest failure of civilization – it constitutes an indelible stain on the fabric of human history. Names like Waterloo, Gettysburg, Bataan, or Normandy all point to the bravery of man – but they also remind us of the savagery that can develop from conflict and that can so characterize human behavior. In many respects, the record of our species is not one of human conflict alone – it's also one of animal ferocity, and in many cases, unspeakable atrocities.

The history of civilization has developed around one indisputable fact: man has always tried to better himself at the expense of his fellow man. That's because we all share common needs for survival, comfort, power, and achievement. Yet the resources available to satisfy these needs are limited. There is only so much food, only so much energy, and only so much wealth. But mankind's desire knows no such limit. And without an endless supply of these resources, the absence of conflict is not likely.

The Darker Side of Human Nature

Desire, violence, and death – these have always been part of the human condition, resulting from the inevitable conflicts of life. More than anything else, any society must learn to deal with these aspects of human nature effectively if it is to survive. That's why strong military power is absolutely essential – not to have the means of destruction but rather to have the means of avoiding destruction.

Those who have spent any time in the wild know that the natural process of resolving conflicts is often very harsh – the only real law that governs conflict in nature is that of survival of the fittest. If an animal can't compete for food, it slowly starves to death, assuming it isn't killed first by an opportunistic predator.

Man, however, has evolved beyond the harshness of natural law. Social order now constrains nature with rules of humanity – rules laced with codes of morality, decency, and honor. That's why we now feed the hungry and care for the sick rather than prey upon them.

The basic laws of nature, however, are still present. They haven't been changed or repealed – only masked or held in check by mankind's desire to grow beyond survival-of-the-fittest behavior. Within each human, no matter how civilized, how decent, or how moral, deep down there's still the savage aspect of personality – one attuned to coping with a harsh, natural environment.

Virtually everywhere we look today we see evidence of this savagery – from the violent crimes that appear daily in a big city's police blotter to the inhumane use of lethal chemical weapons in the hills of Afghanistan or the jungles of Southeast Asia. Documented occurrences of political persecution, torture, and even mass murder attest to man's inhumanity to man – and point to a reality that's not likely to change in the immediate future, if ever.

Many social scientists attribute much of man's belligerent and uncivilized behavior to a part of the brain known as the Reptilian Complex, or R-Complex, because it's a throwback to the ferocity of the early dinosaur. Many scientists believe it's the primary source for anger, rage, and violent action in man today.

Fortunately, for the most part, such behavior is held in check by our ability to reason. But as the destruction that goes on all around us shows, vicious and brutal instincts still exist. To a very real extent, they can still make any of us a victim of our own passions – or the passions of our fellow human beings.

Deterrence and Self-Defense

Historically, man has dealt successfully with the reality of man's savage aspect in one of two ways – either by making himself impregnable against the brutality of others or by having the capability and will to inflict unacceptable damage on such adversaries should they attack. The first approach, that of impregnability, has included such strategies as digging moats around castles or erecting walls around cities – and, for a time, they worked well enough. But as weapons technology advanced, these approaches to self-defense became less effective. Indeed, the day an enemy developed a cannon that could destroy a city's wall, the wall ceased to be a reliable defense.

The second approach to self-defense, that of having the capability and will to inflict unacceptable damage on an enemy, forms the concept of *deterrence*. Deterrence has also been around a long time, but unlike walls and moats, it hasn't been overtaken by modern weapons technology. If anything, it has been enhanced. As technology developed, man's ability to project his power and inflict unacceptable damage on potential adversaries, even after being attacked first, has also increased.

The interesting thing about deterrence is that it only exists in the eye of the beholder. For it to work, an enemy must believe that its potential victim possesses both the capability to inflict unacceptable damage and the will to use this capability. When both are present, history tells us that deterrence does work. It has only been when nations have not possessed the requisite capability or will, or allowed either to weaken, or have ignored the inevitability of conflict and the underlying ferocity of man that they've paid the terrible price of defeat and subjugation: humanity degraded, freedoms forfeited, and life destroyed.

A Case Study of Adolph Hitler

Many studies of human aggression exist today, but perhaps none so telling as those of Adolph Hitler, and the nations, property, and people he destroyed before and during World War II. He laid out his master plan in a book called *Mein Kampf*, but few outside Germany read it or paid much attention to what it said. And even when he began putting his ideas into action, most of the world refused to see the danger or react to it.

In 1933 Hitler removed his country from the League of Nations and walked out of the Geneva Disarmament Conference. This made clear his intent to rearm, but the Allies did nothing. Even though they had the military capability to deter Nazi expansion, they were unable to face the harsh reality and, therefore, lacked the will to use it.

In 1935 Hitler revealed that Germany had secretly built an air force and had provided for an army of 36 divisions. But again the Allies did nothing, because the world was full of too many people who wanted "peace at any price," who were too taken with concerns of cost and humanity to think about fighting a war. Again, the Allies clearly had the capability to stop Hitler. But deterrence failed because Hitler believed the Allies would run away from the problem. And Hitler was right.

The following year, Nazi troops marched into the demilitarized Rhineland, and again the democracies of the world proved incapable of dealing with the problem. Again, Hitler wagered that many of these democracies would prove incapable of even admitting that a problem existed — and, again, Hitler was right.

In subsequent years, Nazi expansion increased. First Austria was victimized, followed by Czechoslovakia. And again, as Hitler predicted, the Allies did not respond. Both France and Britain refused to honor their pledges of support for Czechoslovakia, preferring instead to look the other way and rely on Hitler's humanity. Their inaction effectively removed the last element of deterrence, the last barrier of uncertainty that Hitler could see between himself and the conquest of Europe.

Then there was Poland. Throughout the '30s, Poland looked across its vulnerable plains to the Nazi buildup on three sides. Yet it didn't modernize its antiquated air force, and it did not replace its horse cavalry with armor. Rather, following the now-familiar pattern, it yearned so much for peace that it trusted in Adolph Hitler.

But Hitler wanted Poland, and on September 1, 1939, Hitler brutally and savagely took what he wanted. Of course, he knew this time the Allies would have to fight him, because this time they'd have no choice. But he also knew that, for the Allies, it was already too late. The problem of tyranny had grown too large, their resources were now in short supply, and there was no longer any time. The Nazis were too strong, and although the Allies had finally gained the will to fight, they no longer had the military capability to deter Nazi aggression nor the time to produce it. Thus, the refusal of the world's democracies to face the harsh realities of life led directly to the tragedy of World War II.

The total breakdown of European Allied deterrence first devastated Poland. Fifty-six German divisions, including nine armored, rolled through the Polish countryside, often destroying everything and everyone in their path. And 1500 Luftwaffe warplanes indiscriminately strafed and bombed Poland's cities. The once beautiful and vibrant Warsaw was ultimately reduced to a pitiful collection of burnt buildings, starving and grieving people, and everywhere the smell of death. Finally, with the country in ruins, the Nazis called for the systematic annihilation of Poles, a course of action that ultimately claimed some 5 million lives. Such was the humanity of Adolph Hitler and his Nazi followers. Such was the inherent savagery of man. Such was the price of denying reality.

The French Experience

In 1940 a distinguished historian from the Sorbonne University, Professor Marc Bloch, wrote:

> *The average human being finds in the immediate past a convenient screen to set between himself and the distant truths of history. It keeps him from realizing that the embalmed tragedies of an older day may once again become realities.*

Bloch knew well the harsh realities about which he wrote. As an officer in the French army in 1939, and then, until his death, as a member of the French Resistance, he saw first hand the cost of ignoring distant truths.

After the First World War, France had dominated the European continent. It had won a great victory against Germany and had regained the lost provinces of Alsace and Lorraine. But the lives lost, the material spent, the destruction wrought, the apparent waste of human endeavor – all these things combined to shield the French from the reality of Hitler's National Socialism. As the French people put a few years of peace between them and the First World War, they seemed to cry out, "Never again – at all cost we will avoid future wars." They had experienced the price of victory. But they had yet to experience the much greater price of defeat.

The memory of the Great War controlled how the French people viewed the world. It allowed their fears to determine not only their foreign policy, but ultimately, their military organization and doctrine as well. Both the French people and military took on a defensive strategy – one of containing their potential adversaries and defending vital interests.

Yet the French failed to recognize the fact that only a strong, credible military force, one whose power could be projected wherever needed, would allow their deterrent strategy to succeed. Instead of building such a force, the French emasculated their military by taking away much of its war fighting capability. Like Homer's mariners sailing through Greek mythology, they were lured by the false enticement of the sirens' song, ultimately hiding behind their Maginot Line, an anachronism of escapist mentality.

Before his torture and death at the hands of the Nazis, Marc Bloch wrote a passionate account of the disaster of 1940. His words are not only vivid and moving, but also show perhaps more clearly than most the importance of a strong military to the well-being of a free society – especially one which has adopted a defensive posture.

He tells of that day in Rennes when, to the surprise of everyone, a German column rolled down the boulevard. No one had thought this possible. Yet it was happening, and not a shot was fired. French soldiers and officers just stood by and watched. In addition, he tells of the horrors of the German occupation of France: the loss of France's freedom, the drain on its spirit, and the wholesale destruction and degradation of its humanity.

In France during the 1930s, a variety of social and economic pressures effectively eroded the French military. There was a kind of "rear area mentality." Loss of freedom and life did not seem real possibilities, and the threat seemed to be somewhere else. This attitude is analogous to the sense of security one has in his home during a severe snow storm – that feeling of being safe and snug inside while the storm is raging outside. But anyone who has ever had the electricity fail or the food run out during a blizzard knows full well how false that sense of security can be.

France had been warned: newsreels had shown images of material ruin and inhuman atrocities in both Spain and Poland. Yet many French refused to believe it could happen to them. Years of peace had shielded them from that reality. The storm was outside – yet they were safe and warm behind the false security of an ill-trained, ill-equipped military caught up in its mind-sets of the past. They felt secure, even though their factories were not turning out enough war materiel, even though their workers were more concerned with hourly wages and benefits than with supporting the common defense.

The pacifist movement, often well-meaning but misguided, had taken hold. As Bloch pointed out, more and more people tended not to distinguish between the immorality of a planned war of aggression and the absolute morality of a war imposed on a nation that must react in self defense. French pacifists even went so far as to argue that Hitler was not nearly so bad as he was made out to be. Unfortunately, he turned out to be much worse.

It's worth noting at this point that, like the French of 1939, Americans today also bear their own brand of wartime scars –

scars from the destruction, the demoralization, and the human waste of a war in Southeast Asia, a war we never really tried to win. And like the French, America has also adopted a defensive policy—one of containing the threat and protecting vital national interests.

Is It 1939 Again?

It seems hard to believe that so many free Europeans in the 1930s, having just experienced the pain of World War I, could so easily deny the harsh reality that the Axis powers represented. And it seems even harder to believe that the same thing could happen again, especially to us.

But less than four decades after the end of World War II, the forces of tyranny are again on the move, and those who stand to lose the most, those who are still free, are again denying the harsh reality. Just compare NATO and Warsaw Pact forces today. The Warsaw Pact has over 46,000 main battle tanks; NATO has less than 18,000. The Warsaw Pact has almost 95,000 armored personnel carriers; NATO has less than 40,000. The Warsaw Pact has 6000 transport/support helicopters; NATO has less than 1400.

In 1984, the Soviet Union produced 100 new ICBMs, while NATO produced none; the Soviets produced 350 short-range ballistic missiles, while NATO produced none; and in terms of sea-launched ballistic missiles, the Soviets produced 200, while NATO produced only 80.

By 1985, the Soviet Union had expanded its military capability to the extent where, when compared with the United States, it had deployed a third-more ICBMs, but with almost five times the number of reentry vehicles. It had also deployed two and a half times the number of sea-launched ballistic missiles.

Yet during these years, even with the evidence at hand, Americans argued incessantly over the defense budget. They evaluated how large it should be, questioned the strategic deterrent force we maintain, asked whether it should be upgraded—and too many searched for ways to do without defense altogether.

As we debated in virtually every public forum how the MX should be based, or even whether it should be built at all, the

Soviets modernized their ICBM force and began testing new ICBM systems. And as Americans argued the merits of building the B-1B, the Soviets continued development of their new generation strategic bomber, the Blackjack, which is larger than the B-1B.

As Americans debated the need for increased intermediate-range nuclear forces, the Soviets were greatly expanding their intermediate nuclear capability, adding hundreds of mobile launchers and deploying advanced warplanes to Eastern Europe and border bases in Asia.

As Americans questioned the need for a strengthened U.S. Navy, the Soviets were making their third new Kiev-class aircraft carrier operational, and they were continuing development on a newer and larger nuclear-powered aircraft carrier. Additionally, both their Baltic and Black Sea shipyards were producing four new classes of surface warships, while five Soviet shipyards were turning out new attack submarines for what was then the world's largest submarine force.

As Americans argued about the morality of war, the Soviets were making war – deploying more than 100,000 troops in Afghanistan, testing some of their latest weapons, including chemical and biological weapons, on the Afghan people, and shooting down an unarmed civilian airliner.

And as Americans in the academic community argued against defense research and development, the Soviets were continuing their intense efforts to improve their technology base. They built the world's largest research and development manpower base, estimated at nearly a million scientists and engineers, and they put 50 to 75 percent of them directly into defense-related work. And in one year alone, the Soviets and other Warsaw Pact nations built half again as many fighters and fighter bombers, almost twice as many sea-launched ballistic missiles, and eight times as many surface to air missiles as compared with the United States and NATO countries.

The Nuclear Freeze Issue

In the second century A.D., Ptolemy devised a model of the universe, one in which the sun and other planets circled the earth.

His idea permitted accurate predictions of planetary motion, and it won enthusiastic support, even of the Church. On the surface, the Ptolemaic model made a lot of sense, and it seemed to work. But in reality it was a misconception, one that not only misled the best minds of Ptolemy's day but also prevented humanity from seeing the truth for another 1300 years.

H. L. Mencken once wrote, "For every problem there is one solution which is simple, neat, and wrong." Putting the earth at the center of the universe was such a solution. It seemed so simple and so obvious that it had to be right. So is the idea of freezing the production of nuclear weapons. In recent years, many Americans, including many political and religious leaders, have demonstrated their desire for a simple and neat solution to the modern-day threat of nuclear war. Like Ptolemy's universe, the freeze solution seems simple and neat, and on the surface, it appears quite plausible. But unfortunately, it just won't work. If anything, it will only blind us to a truth we must see and therefore increase the dangers we face.

The arguments in favor of a nuclear freeze are both powerful and attractive. After all, if one warhead can destroy an entire Soviet city, why do we need more warheads than they have cities? Why must we continue to deplete our national resources if we already have sufficient numbers of warheads to deter Soviet nuclear aggression? Surely, with our land-based ICBM's, our fleet of nuclear bombers, and our missile-carrying submarines roaming deep beneath the seas, we'd have enough retaliatory punch left after any Soviet aggression to deter that aggression in the first place.

If that were so, the freeze might not be a bad idea. But our retaliatory capability is now in serious question. In past years, the Soviets have made vast improvements in accuracy and explosive power, and they've produced thousands of modern, nuclear warheads. Compared to the Soviets, we've done little in the past decade to upgrade our strategic deterrent — our triad of land-based missiles, submarine-launched missiles, and manned bombers. We've seriously neglected the only real defense we've ever had against the power arrayed against us.

A Deteriorating Deterrent

During the '70s, we restrained our deployment of new systems. The Soviets took advantage of our efforts to slow the nuclear arms race by building at least 10 variations of three new ICBM's – modern, powerful, and accurate offensive weapons designed to destroy us and our democracy. We, on the other hand, deployed no new ICBM's and only one variation of a missile we already had. The trends shown in Figure 3 demonstrate our changing strategic position vis-à-vis the Soviets.

Our 1000 or so land-based missiles are today vulnerable to a Soviet first strike. Using only part of their modern ICBM force, the Soviets now have the capability to destroy a large percentage of our land-based missile deterrent.

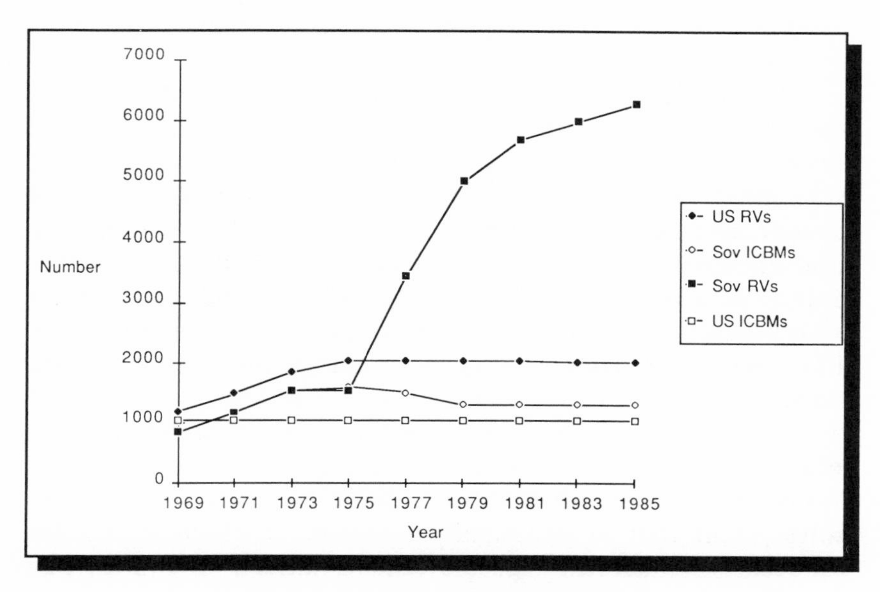

Fig. 3. U.S. and Soviet ICBM Launcher and Reentry Vehicle (RV) Deployment 1969-1985.
(Data from Soviet Military Power, *4th ed., Washington, D.C.: U.S. Government Printing Office, April 1985, p. 30.)*

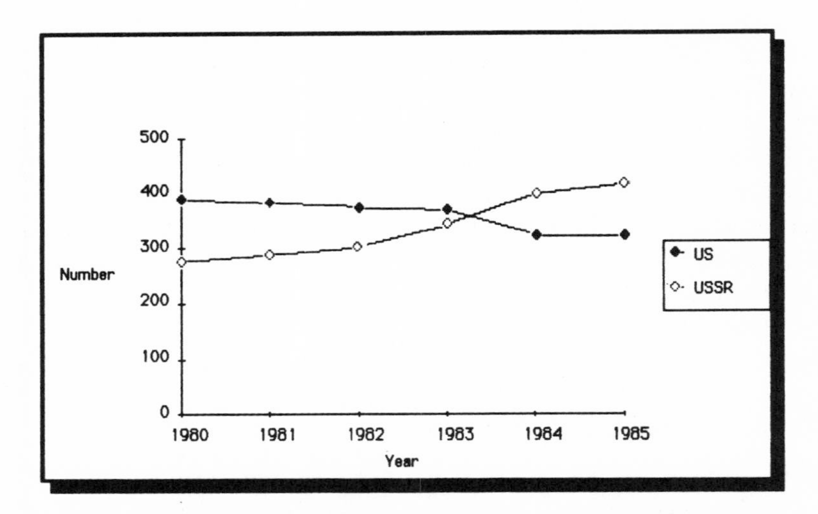

Fig. 4. U.S. and Soviet Intercontinental-Capable Bombers.
(Data from Soviet Military Power*, 4th ed., Washington, D.C.: U.S. Government Printing Office, April 1985, p. 34.)*

What about our strategic bombers? Today we rely on the B-52 to penetrate Soviet air defenses. But as Figure 4 shows, our strategic bomber position has also weakened in recent years. Moreover, we have come to rely on an airplane that's older than the crews who fly it. The newest B-52 was built in 1962, and although we've updated its electronic systems, we haven't changed its shape or size. And that's really the rub. Its shape and size will soon make it too susceptible to enemy radar and associated air defenses.

Finally, what about our missile-carrying submarines? Although the comparison of submarine launched ballistic missiles and reentry vehicles in Figure 5 looks relatively favorable, our nuclear submarines cannot alone provide us the deterrent we need. For one thing, the accuracy of a submarine-launched missile is not anywhere as good as the accuracy of land-based missiles. And without the pin-point accuracy of our land-based missiles and manned-bombers, we could not preclude a Soviet second strike.

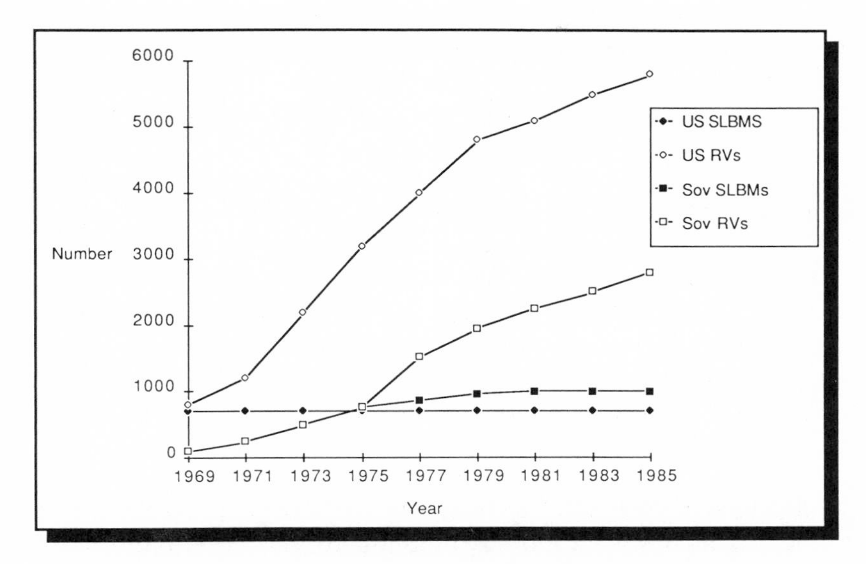

Fig. 5. U.S. and Soviet SLBM Launcher and Reentry Vehicle (RV) Deployment 1969-1985.
(Data from Soviet Military Power, *4th ed., Washington, D.C.: U.S. Government Printing Office, April 1985, p. 33.)*

Secondly, although submarines at sea are considered invulnerable to a Soviet first strike, antisubmarine warfare technology is evolving very fast. Consequently, there no longer may be the guarantee that our strategic triad's third element will survive such a strike. And if the Soviets only have our submarine-launched missiles to deal with, they'll have that many more resources with which to do the job. Consider also the age of our submarine fleet: it was only in the last couple of years that we began to launch new missile-firing submarines, our first in a decade and a half.

In effect, a freeze would open us up to nuclear blackmail. Given a Soviet first strike, there's no guarantee that we'd have the wherewithal to prevent a second strike. And if we couldn't prevent a second strike, just what would we do after a first strike? Would we launch what we have left, senselessly killing millions of noncombatant Soviet citizens? Would we be willing then to lay ourselves open for the devastating Soviet second strike that would certainly follow? Or would we give in? Would we forfeit for our children what 200 years of sacrifice and determination have given us? And if we did give in, what price would we have to pay?

Lessons of the Past Unlearned

In considering tough issues like the nuclear freeze, it's important that we remember how savage man can be, and how inevitable conflict is. It's important that we remember that we are an honorable, peace-loving people who scorn aggression, who live by their word, and who will not start a war. And it's important that we remember that this puts us at a decided disadvantage.

Many Americans want a nuclear freeze because they want to reduce the danger of nuclear war. Yet historically, unilateral disarmament, which is what a freeze amounts to, has never reduced the chance of war. It has only increased it. A freeze on our part today would represent a shrinking from the responsibility of being free, a shrinking not unlike that which characterized Europe in the 1930s. Many members of the free world, including many Americans, seem little inclined to face the unpleasant facts in the world around them. Yet mankind's history is there for all to see, and its lessons should be easy enough to learn.

In our modern, civilized world, many fail to understand the real nature of international power. They don't see that nations have vital interests that they'll pursue using economic, political, diplomatic, demographic, and military means. They don't recognize that some nations subscribe to the thesis that the more willing and capable a country is to pursue its aims with blatant and inhuman military force, the less complicated and demanding its course will be.

Other nations such as the United States pursue their national goals and protect their vital interests in a different way, in a manner consistent with their values and beliefs. Such nations respect the dignity and humanity of all mankind. Consequently, they must shoulder the extra burden and have that extra measure of international credibility that can only come from a believable and plausible armed force. That may well be a sad commentary on the nature of humanity, but that is, in fact, the way it is – and the way it has always been. A strong military capability is one of the major prices we must pay for being a free and decent people.

The American military-industrial complex is the war-fighting arm of our free society. Historically, the defense establishment has not been associated with the nicer things in life, but rather it has often been associated with death, destruction, war, and violence. The irony, of course, is that without a strong, credible armed force, we as a free people could accomplish very little good in the world. Without such a force, we as a free people would not even exist.

Emasculating the American Military

It's truly amazing what a few years of peace and prosperity have done to the thought processes of many people. The years since World War II have provided that convenient screen Marc Bloch wrote about – the one that can filter out unpleasant truths. More and more, Americans are becoming infatuated with the good things in life. Less and less do they readily admit to the harsh realities inherent in human existence. And since the military is so closely associated with these unpleasantries, less and less do they tolerate their own military.

Since World War II, when some 15 million civilians entered our armed forces, there's been an unabated effort to normalize the military, to make it less distinctive as a war-fighting organization – and thus, to make it a less visible reminder of that which many seek to deny. Today we've even changed its name: we don't have a War Department any more – we have a Defense Department; and we don't fight wars any more – we engage in conflicts or even police actions.

Society also tries to normalize the military by thinking of it in nonmilitary terms. For example, more and more we seem to think of military people as a group of federal employees with a particular job description. We compare the military's functions with those of the civilian sector. We compare the two in terms of efficiency; we compare their remuneration in terms of pay and benefits; we compare their job skills in terms of relative education level and importance; and we compare their daily lives in terms of work hours and paid vacations.

Yet we fail to recognize one important truth: there is no civilian counterpart for the military part of the defense equation. Civilian and military functions are not comparable. If they were, we wouldn't need a specialized, disciplined group of dedicated people to fight our battles for us.

The cumulative effect of comparing military with civilian and of managing the military function as a civilian enterprise can be devastating to any military's ability to perform its combat role. Such societal pressures over the years may have substantially weakened this nation's armed forces and may have reduced their credibility around the world.

This is especially true if one factors into the defense equation our reduced military spending during the past two decades. Until fiscal year 1981, defense spending, as a function of real dollars, was lower than 1962 levels. On the average, except for the Vietnam buildup, the defense budget declined from 1962 to 1982.

Many look back at the "golden days" of the late Kennedy and early Johnson years and yearn to go back. They yearn to return to that time when, they believe, we had our priorities straight – when we had defense in its proper, subordinate place. Yet they're shielding themselves from facts – they're hiding from the reality that those were the days when we spent a much larger share of our nation's resources on defense. Between 1964 and 1979, we reduced defense spending from 8 percent to 5 percent of our nation's GNP.

The Real Concern

The real concern is this: historically, whenever a free nation has emasculated its military because of the unpleasant associations of death and war or the apparent drain on national resources – whenever it has compromised the military's weapon systems or the means of producing them, reduced its national support, or discouraged its dedicated personnel – that country has lost not only its international credibility, but more often than not, it has wound up going to war. And frequently, it has paid a far more grievous price than ever thought possible – by losing that war.

There are fewer and fewer people in this country who lived through World War II and its prelude. For those who did, it was a period of dark tyrannies, psychological denial, and of many nations' paying a grievous price. What happened was not fiction. It was real. And the screaming and the crying and the pain were real.

But the harsh truths of those days have, for most, been relegated to the pages of history. Some no longer believe in the savagery of man, others no longer acknowledge the existence of tyranny, and perhaps most are no longer willing to face the danger that threatens them. They have fallen victim to that same *rear-area* mentality that leads to denial of the unpleasant, even at the expense of all logic or reason.

They're repulsed by the waste and carnage of war and rightly so. But they respond by denying its possibility and by striking out irrationally at its most visible symbol: the military-industrial complex. They fail to see that the tranquility of their countryside or the commerce of their city all depend on this country's having an effective, war-fighting capability.

The real question today is whether it's 1939 again. The parallels between today's America and the France of 1939 are striking and disturbing. But there is one important difference. By the time 1939 had come, and the winds of war were blowing, France's fate was sealed. It had had the resources and know-how to defend itself, but it had not chosen to do so – and by 1939, it was too late.

We, on the other hand, still control our destiny. Clearly this country has the resources (albeit limited), and it has the talent and the desire to be free. Furthermore, we Americans still have enough time – but perhaps not much more than that. Thus we have the wherewithal to maintain a strong and credible defense, and, as in World War II, we are mankind's last real hope for freedom. The decision is still ours. It will be the decision that determines whether mankind continues to have a meaningful existence on this planet.

CHAPTER 4

Mind-Sets and Difficult Problems

Each scientific discipline has a pattern for viewing the cosmos, a mind-set that not only provides a structure and framework for thought but also constrains the thought process itself. For example, Newton's physical laws governed for many years how people thought about the movement of objects – and most found it impossible to conceive of a reality not premised on these basic laws. Then Einstein proposed a different reality, one that warped the normal concepts of space and distance with a fourth dimension of time. Today, of course, physicists readily accept Einstein's theory and use it as the current mind-set to study the universe.

During the 1930s, the French viewed national defense much the same way scientists once viewed Newtonian physics: They were convinced of the correctness of their position and could not conceive of a reality that differed. In effect, they were caught in the grips of an outdated mind-set. Thus they were blinded not only to the dangers they faced but to the ways of best allocating the resources they had to deal effectively with these dangers.

In terms of our national defense, we may well be experiencing the same phenomenon today. It's incredible how many resources we may waste, how many problems we may not be able to fully solve, and how much excellence we may not achieve – simply because we fail to exploit the latest technology, because we fail to take advantage of powerful solutions that are often readily available to us for the taking. In effect, we often fail to see such solutions simply because we're screened from them by our mind-sets from the past.

The Mind-Set Problem

Mind-sets are internalized patterns of human perception. They are structured ways of viewing various realities — ways developed as a result of experience, education, and maturation within a particular group.

Mind-sets often can be very useful. They may provide for more efficient human functioning, since they establish beforehand the basic rules of this functioning. As long as mind-sets accurately reflect the reality of the environment in which they exist, they are a positive influence on human behavior.

But when mind-sets based on out-of-date realities continue in force, they no longer serve any useful function and, more often than not, cause significant problems of human perception. A good example of the effects of a dysfunctional mind-set can be found with the plight of the American auto industry during the '70s. In the early '70s, American automakers' had a perceptual framework for viewing cars — one that focused on power, luxury, and large size.

But then, in 1973-74, when gasoline became scarce and expensive, reality changed. But the mind-set based on a then outdated environmental truth — that is, plentiful, inexpensive energy — continued to control the automakers' perceptions. It wasn't until the '80s that they accepted the true economic realities. Only then did they reorient themselves to a new mind-set of economy and reliability.

Mind-Sets and the Military

The U.S. military is no exception to the mind-set problem. It too is plagued by dysfunctional mind-sets, many of which date back to the late 1940s. Those were the days when we relied on paper pads, wooden pencils, and single-button telephones. Things moved more slowly back then: information was sent by cable, often by telegraphic code, and military operations progressed at a snail's pace by modern standards.

But today that's all changed. For one thing, this nation is no longer an island unto itself. Many of our vital resources, like energy (oil and gas), strategic materials (titanium, chromium, cobalt, and so on), and critical processes (electronic manufacturing and assembly), come from the far reaches of the globe, often from unfriendly suppliers and often over easily interdicted supply lines. As Table 1 shows, our overseas dependencies for a single jet engine type alone are significant.

Table 1. Imported Metals for the F100 Jet Engine.

Metal	Lbs Per Engine*	% Imported	Sources
Nickel	4504	68	Canada, USSR, Australia
Chromium	1485	77	S. Africa, USSR, Zimbabwe
Titanium	5440	95	Australia, S. Africa (Rutile)
Cobalt	885	97	Zaire, Zambia
Columbium	145	100	Brazil, Canada, Thailand
Tantalum	3	92	Canada, Zaire, Indonesia

*Input Weight Requirement

Source: Pratt & Whitney, United Technologies, 1986: Mel Siegel, Consultant, P&W-GPD Materials, Using 1985 Bureau of Mines Data

This table demonstrates the foreign dependencies that exist just for those strategic materials required in the production of the F100 jet engine – the engine used on our first-line air superiority fighter, the F-15, and our first line air-to-ground fighter, the F-16. This data represents just the tip of the iceberg of how dependent our combat capability is on outside and often unfriendly or distant sources of supply.

Additionally, many more nations, including many emerging nations, now have modern military technology. They now have the capability to seriously threaten, at the source, many of the energy supplies, strategic materials, and critical processes our society has come to rely on.

One other thing has changed: the speed at which events unfold. Senior military planners now must cope with scenarios like the *come-as-you-are war* – a conflict that can start suddenly and unpredictably in remote areas and grow to significant levels of intensity virtually overnight. Such an event may seriously threaten our vital interests.

The elements of warfare also move much faster. Modern forces can be projected thousands of miles in a matter of hours, while command, control, and intelligence information is routinely transmitted around the world at the speed of light by satellites. Operations are measured in nanoseconds or microseconds. In effect, real time has speeded up.

How well is the military organized to deal in real time? For years now, we've allowed our mind-sets of the past to blind us to realities of the present. Just consider that much of our military organization and procedure is based on the truths of the late '40s, when there was a scarcity of expertise and experience in the military. Most of those who served before World War II left the service at war's end. Those who came in immediately preceding and during the war were relatively young. They lacked the education and experience needed to field and manage the large force required to deal with the emerging Soviet threat. With the relatively crude communications and transportation systems of that period, those who were qualified had to be clustered in major command headquarters, where they could direct the activities of everyone else.

Today we don't have that problem. The military has plenty of competent people, along with the technology to communicate and travel quickly. Yet much of it is still organized to deal in the time frame of the '40s and '50s. It still has basically the same major command structure as it had then, and the headquarters of these commands still tend to direct the operation. The result: the military is not fully capitalizing on the talent to lead and manage now available throughout the force.

Also consider how the military must do business today. Following outdated mind-sets, it still must look ahead 10 years or so, predict what the situation will be, then limit capability to what had been predicted. But doing that doesn't make good sense anymore – especially considering the track record in predicting the future. For example, in 1970 we foresaw continued hostility with China, but expected to rely on our close friendship with Iran and our unlimited supply of inexpensive oil from the Middle East. But the reality we had to deal with ten years later, in 1980, was quite different from what we expected.

Clearly military planning must be dynamic — it must be capable of responding quickly to the unexpected, because the unexpected in the past has usually been the reality we've faced. The military actions we take must be more responsive to planning, planning must be more responsive to what we're capable of doing, and both must be more responsive to the environment.

The best way to do this is to have a dynamic operation that integrates planning, programming, budgeting, and implementation into some type of single, functional model. Within this model, all key decision-making elements would interact, so that any changes anywhere in the system or in the environment could be reflected and updated continuously.

Yet today the military must still do business the old way — it is still constrained with budget and planning cycles that are totally inconsistent with the dynamic, fast changing environment around us. At a minimum, the military must get relief from the straight-jacket of the currently mandated annual programming and budgeting cycle. Needed instead is a system capable of adjusting as dictated by fact-of-life situations, albeit within some broad and general budgetary guidelines.

Mind-Sets and the Defense Industry

The mind-set problems briefly discussed in the examples so far have an obvious impact on our ability to defend our nation. But perhaps nowhere is the mind-set problem more serious than in the way our defense industrial base is set up to provide the military with combat capability. For more than anywhere else in the defense equation, we're still living in the past in the area of weapons procurement and support. We don't do things differently today. We do them just like we did them decades ago — in another day and another age.

Much of our present defense industrial base was set up in the 1940s. Certainly no one can deny that this system worked well then. One need only look at the production achievements of World War II. In 44 months, the defense industry produced 310,000 aircraft, 88,000 tanks, 411,000 artillery pieces, 900,000 military trucks, 358 destroyers, 211 submarines, 27 aircraft carriers, and 10 battleships.

But the important question now is not what we did in World War II. It's what we can do today. If we're honest with ourselves, we'd have to admit that we can't even produce what we need today, much less what we'd need in time of war. And we certainly can't begin to match our accomplishment of yesteryear.

Just consider that producing a B-1 bomber takes about 15 years from inception to first significant delivery. Sure, many would argue that political delays, funding delays, and research and development take their toll — but that's the point. Such delays are a reality of our modern environment. They grow from our dependence on ultra-sophisticated technology and from a lack of sustained commitment to defense or from the reluctance or inability of the federal government to pay the price.

In World War II, one of our strategic bombers, the B-24, cost us $336,000 a copy — and we built 10,000 in just three years. At the same time, we were building hundreds of thousands of other aircraft. Consider the P-51, the plane that proved so valuable in defeating enemy fighter aircraft. During World War II, we built 15,000 P-51s, or over 4000 per year. Today we rely on the F-15 to clear the skies of enemy fighters. Yet these days, we produce only about 95 F-15s annually. Under wartime conditions using our limited surge capability, we might squeeze out a few more.

But what if that is not enough? Where will adequate numbers of modern systems come from? Looking through the rose-colored lenses of past mind-sets, we seem to believe that American industry can and will do the job for us as it did in World War II. But the evidence says otherwise. Look at the industrial base we must depend on for our survival.

The fact is that the great Arsenal of Democracy of the 1940s has withered, a victim of one of the lowest rates of investment in new plants and equipment of all industrialized countries — a victim of disincentives, especially in aerospace and defense industries, a victim of a system where increased productivity does not benefit industry, but in fact, often results in a reduction of after-tax profit. But more than anything else, it has been a victim of changing times and mind-sets that haven't kept pace.

Weapons Procurement: A Historical Perspective

The history of weapon system procurement in the military since World War II consists of two distinct periods. In the early period, immediately following the war and continuing throughout the '50s, there was virtually no resource the military could not control, and no industrial might it could not command. At the time, to deter the growing Soviet threat and to keep up with rapidly evolving aerospace technology, the military embarked on a truly remarkable program of new system development.

Consider strategic bomber production. In 1945, of course, we relied on the B-29. But within two years, we were already producing the B-36, a bomber that could meet the new requirement of flying three times as far, 25 percent higher, with four times the payload.

But even as the military began taking deliveries on the B-36, it was testing a pure jet bomber. With rapidly advancing technology, we could ill afford relying on a deterrent force that couldn't effectively penetrate to the target. That's why, by 1951, the military started receiving some 2000 B-47s, that could cruise two and a half times faster than the B-36. Within another year, the first of over 800 B-52s appeared on the scene, because already the military foresaw the need for a plane that could fly 10,000 feet higher than the B-47 and carry four times as many bombs.

This early period was characterized by the development of hundreds of new systems, from aircraft carriers to tanks. The Air Force received not only its strategic bomber force but also the Century Series Fighters, various air transports, and the Atlas, Titan, and Minuteman missiles.

In those days the defense industry was healthy. Production

lines were always warm — as soon as one project was completed, another one took its place. This was the time when our present-day mind-sets were formed.

Then, starting in the early '60s and extending through the '70s, we moved into the second period of modern weapons procurement. The resources required to support evolving technology began to far outstrip what we were willing or capable of investing. Suddenly new system production dropped off to a trickle. Increasingly, we took the more economical approach of modifying our present systems to give them new capability.

The last B-52 was delivered in 1962, and a quarter century will have passed before its replacement, the B-1B, is operationally ready. During the 1970s, we deployed no new ICBM types and only a single variant of an existing system. And it wasn't until 1982 that we finally commissioned a new Trident submarine, our first new system of that kind in 15 years.

Of course, we are building a few new systems now — but not nearly in the numbers we used to. For one thing, to some extent, we don't need to, because the power of modern technology will allow us to do more with less. And for another, we probably couldn't afford to build modern systems in those large numbers anyway — not when an F-15 fighter costs $22 million, not when a new C-5B transport costs $150 million, not when a B-1B costs $200 million. Because of price tags like these, we're no longer buying systems that we'll use and replace. Today we're investing, literally, in national assets, systems that probably will be in the inventory for another quarter century or longer.

A Change in Priorities

The implications of current realities for the military, and particularly for the Air Force (given rapid advances in aerospace technology) are substantial, especially considering present mind-sets. The most obvious implication, of course, is that we won't be building as many new weapon systems[1] in the future. More and more, we'll be finding ways to update what we have with new technology. More and more, the maintenance and improvement of our present systems will be a top priority.

This new approach is especially likely in areas where digital electronics have replaced, or will replace, electro-mechanical devices. In many cases, digital devices do not need to be rebuilt when they become outdated; they need only be reprogrammed. That's why military planners expect software redevelopment (the updating and writing of computer program codes) to become a prime determinant of our combat capability.

Some studies predict the number of computers embedded in weapon systems will increase at least 25 times by the 1990s, with computer costs rising an order of magnitude or more. But, importantly, it's possible that only about 15 percent of what we'll spend on computers by 1990 will be on hardware. Software, particularly software redevelopment, will be the real source of improvements in combat capability.

What are the implications of all this for our nation's defense industry? Keeping weapon systems longer and modifying them as needed is without doubt an effective way to generate new combat capability. But what does reliance on computers and software do to the industrial base of the country? What impact does this approach have on our ability to support these weapon systems in their mature years — years when such support is perhaps most critical?

Between 1967 and 1980, we lost almost half our dedicated defense contractors. Fewer than 3500 remained in business by 1981. In some areas, this attrition was critical. For example, we were down to one producer of precision ball bearings for military air frames and only three suppliers of the large forgings for aircraft ribs.

Now not only is our capacity to support wartime production suspect, but what capacity we do have is also too dependent on foreign suppliers. Just consider the migration of the electronics industry to foreign countries. We have no backup production capability in this country for many of our electronic imports. We've forfeited it to more competitive, more productive overseas suppliers.

We've also lost much of our skilled defense work force. Some types of electronic component assembly are almost exclusively performed overseas now. During times of war, this supply of skilled labor is eminently interruptible. The defense industry recruits only one-fourth of the 10,000 machinists needed each year. In addition, the defense industry needs about 75,000 engineers per year, but our colleges and universities graduate only about two-thirds that number. And that's not all. By the early '80s, we had shortfalls of almost 50 percent in computer specialists and almost 85 percent in statisticians. These were and are very critical skills.

Work force inadequacies pose a very serious threat to our security. If an emergency arises, things aren't going to work as they did in World War II. No longer can we recruit farmers, clerks, and housewives and put them to work in our defense factories – not building F-15s and F-16s. Technology is too advanced, tolerances are too tight, and the specialized skills are too hard to acquire.

We're also not going to be able to convert from commercial production to wartime production as we did in World War II. In the first place, we may not have the strategic materials needed to even begin production. For example, one engine manufacturer splits its work about 50-50 between military and commercial markets. But if it turns to more military production, just where's the titanium and other scarce materials needed in military programs going to come from?

It's a fact that we no longer have an Arsenal of Democracy to support us in the type of conflicts that are becoming evermore likely – the come-as-you-are war scenario discussed earlier. We won't have years to mobilize as we did in World War II. We may be more likely to have days or at best a few weeks. And given this reality, any hope that America's defense industry as presently structured can meet our wartime requirements is a pipe dream – one built around mind-sets from the past.

Adapting to Modern Realities

One way of adapting would be to buy all we'd need to fight a war and store it on the shelf somewhere. Of course, we'd have to come up with a substantial amount of money to finance such an effort. And we'd have to hope that what we bought wouldn't become outdated with the passage of time, that it would be the right thing should war come, and that a war different from what we expected wouldn't deplete our stocks prematurely. Obviously, this is a very risky, very costly, and consequently, a very unacceptable approach.

Another way to approach the problem is to stockpile enough to meet the initial surge of a high-intensity war and then somehow maintain the industrial capability to gear up production rapidly. The problem here, of course, is somewhat the same: how much and what do we stockpile? And how do we maintain the kind of industrial capacity we'd need? We'd probably need it early on — either because we can't afford to stockpile too much, or because we're afraid of stockpiling outdated weapons.

There are two traditional alternatives for defense production. We can do as we have always done and give free enterprise virtually all of the responsibility. Or the government can do the whole job, as the Soviet government does.

The arsenal approach, where government designs and builds weapons, would certainly keep our production capability ready. But how about innovation, that special Yankee ingenuity America is so noted for? From where will we get the technological advances in the future that have kept us free in the past?

But if we leave the entire responsibility for our defense production in the hands of private enterprise, we may not get what we need when we need it. Because of the episodic nature of defense purchases — cyclical patterns of feast or famine in our defense industry — the ability to operate at a profit is chancy at best. Contract winners often win big, but contract losers far more often lose big. And, as we saw in the '70s when we didn't think we needed as much defense, the number of big losers increases dramatically during lean years.

Here's the problem: To defend our nation, we must have an industrial base capable of producing sufficient numbers of reliable weapon systems quickly and affordably. But because of the changes that have occurred since World War II, we're buying fewer, more expensive and more capable new systems. Yet our defense industry still functions under mind-sets built around new-system production. Decades ago, new-system design and procurement grew steadily. Today, with a smaller new-system market, it is difficult, if not impossible, to maintain a healthy and viable defense industry — one which, through keen competition in the free-enterprise system, can continue to supply us with the combat capability we must have.

Parts Pricing: One Indicator of the Problem

Those defense parts-pricing problems so heralded in the press in recent years are in fact just the tip of the iceberg, a single indicator that evidences a much larger problem underneath. Many of those large cost increases can be directly traced to the starving out of private defense contractors, and the loss of skilled people in and out of government. And ultimately, they can be attributed to a decaying competitive environment that undermines the principal strength of our free-enterprise system and compromises the great advantage our society possesses.

Of course, the military did put many fixes into place to deal with the parts-pricing problem, and these are discussed in a later chapter. But so far, our society has basically ignored the more generic industrial base problem and the powerful mind-sets that have really allowed the situation to develop in the first place. Old mind-sets have blinded us to the reality that we're dealing not just with a parts-pricing problem, but with a far more serious malady that has infected our whole defense industry — an industry designed and built decades ago around the outdated concept of constant, steady growth in new-system design and procurement.

A Viable Solution

The real solution, the one that, in the long term, would best use the resources available, is the solution that attacks the real cause: outdated mind-sets. Specifically, the solution would be to update our view of the defense industry to reflect modern realities. We must recast our system so that it is keyed to these realities, not to those of yesteryear. To do that, we must first recognize the long pole in the tent of combat capability for what it has become and then provide the proper incentives to allow private industry to reorient itself around this pole, not around the one which existed decades ago.

In the past, large numbers of new systems were the name of the game. Today, it's smaller numbers of more capable new systems and the updating of existing systems. In addition, we must deal with the new reality that modern, sophisticated weapons rely on modern, sophisticated support to be effective. In the past, support concerns were tangential to the mainstream of our defense effort, especially when we were building and replacing so many systems so fast. Today, however, support is at the very heart of our defense capability — especially considering how much new systems cost, and how long they will remain in the inventory.

The central importance of many support items to the operation of entire systems cannot be overemphasized. In many cases, not having an engine, a spare part, or a piece of test equipment where and when it's needed translates into not having the entire weapon system — just as surely as if it had been destroyed in combat. Support then, not new weapons production, is fast becoming the basis of our military capability.

We need, therefore, to shed the mind-set of the postwar era and get away from thinking only in terms of new systems. And that, more than anything else, requires we take on a whole new mind-set — one that views defense in terms of total capability: new technology leading to new systems that are supportable in the environment in which they will have to operate.

[1]The term *weapon system*, as used here, does not include *smart* munitions like the Cruise Missile. For the most part, such munitions require a weapon system for delivery to the target.

CHAPTER 5

The Logistics Problem

The last chapter focused on mind-sets for the defense industry and new-system acquisition. But perhaps nowhere have mind-sets so affected our ability to defend this nation as in the area of support, or logistics. Of course, logistics has always been the counterpart to strategy and tactics. It is the support arm that made weapon systems effective and that governed, in turn, what strategies could be developed and what tactics could be employed. Logistics has always been basically a science of resource allocation – and that's how we've tended to view it all along.

The problem is that the logistics mind-sets that developed during and after World War II came from an era when we had far more resources than requirements. Our natural resources gave us all the energy we needed, our industrial might gave us all the production capacity we needed, and our geographical isolation gave us all the time we needed.

Logistics was a subordinate concern to strategy and tactics – not because it was really subordinate, but because national security policy and requirements for supporting weapon systems were more limited, and the resources to meet these requirements were in far greater supply. Most people in the defense business never thought much about logistics, because it was a given. That's why, over time, they lost sight of what logistics is all about.

Logistics: Not a Mysterious Process

To understand the magnitude of the logistics problem, it's first necessary to understand what logistics is. But that shouldn't be too hard, even though many people view it as a mysterious process. The plain truth is that anyone functioning in society today probably already knows what logistics is, because just to get along these days requires one to be an experienced logistician.

Think about what you did this morning when you got up. After the clock radio went off, you washed, put on your clothes, and ate breakfast. Pretty straightforward – right? Maybe so, but from a logistician's perspective, it wasn't that simple. What you really did was satisfy a complex set of personal requirements for consumable and reparable products, using an elaborate logistics support process embedded in the economy of our society.

For example, that clock radio was initially manufactured, then purchased, and transported to your bedroom in response to your personal needs through an interdependent system of wholesale-retail outlets. And the electricity that powered the radio was generated and distributed through a sophisticated network of power plants and local utility companies.

Now think of the goods and services you may have relied on during those few minutes you spent washing. Think of the consumables alone – the hot water, electricity, tooth paste, shaving cream, razor blades, light bulbs, soap bars, paper towels, and various lotions, creams, and powders. And think how dependent you were on those items' being at hand. What if there were no hot water, or what if you were out of soap? Or what if the only light in the bathroom had burned out and you didn't have a spare bulb?

But it's not only goods we're dependent on. We also need the services provided by various maintenance activities – services that would become very important if, say, the furnace quit on a cold and blustery night or a water pipe in the basement suddenly burst.

Of course, many such breakdowns in personal logistics have happened to all of us at one time or another. And to one degree or another, they've been infuriating, frustrating, and even dangerous. But they serve to remind us just how dependent on others we are for everyday goods and services.

As members of a consuming society, we all depend substantially on the productivity of others for the clothes we wear, the food we eat, the books we read, and the energy we use. It would be very difficult to find any American who produces even a fraction of his or her basic needs today. That's why it would be virtually impossible to find any American not intimately involved with the process of logistics.

Logistics is simply the supplying of goods and services to where they're needed, when they're needed – whether it be food on the breakfast table when you get up in the morning or fuel in the tank when you drive to work. There is no mystery surrounding logistics – no secret handshake among "loggies" – no confidential code that can't be broken. In a very real sense, we are all experienced logisticians. Without logistics in modern society, there would be no society.

Logistics and the Environment

To really understand what logistics is today, we have to be aware of the environment. The environment not only determines, to a great extent, what goods and services are necessary, but also controls how fast they must be supplied and what means are available to supply them.

The one thing in the environment that has had the greatest effect on logistics is technology. When technology was simple, logistics was simple. To get along in life, early human beings needed only a few basic things: one or two crude weapons for hunting and self-protection, some tools to build and cook with, and maybe a piece of flint to start a fire. They didn't worry about toiletries, light bulbs, and electricity, because they weren't reliant on them.

But technology tends to breed upon itself. Technology's very existence creates a dependency, which, in turn, sets up the need for more technology. Thus technology increases exponentially, along with a similar increase in the need to support this technology – or, in other words, an increasing reliance on logistics.

Consider the computer. Beginning in the late '40s, we started developing computers to store, manipulate, and communicate data faster and more accurately than possible either manually or mechanically. Then, with the discovery of solid-state devices, particularly large-scale integrated circuits, computer technology expanded rapidly, diffusing throughout our society.

Data networks were born — and mainframes, terminals, and stand-alone microcomputers suddenly became important in our daily lives. Then, very quickly, we became reliant on these machines for everything, from communication to word processing, from data storage to video games. Just like hot running water and soap in the bathroom, we can no longer get by without them.

Try to imagine a bank or a brokerage house trying to function now without computers. The manual way of doing business would no longer work in today's real-time world of financial management. If a large commercial bank's computer goes down for even 5 or 10 minutes, disorder and loss of productivity result.

Technology has affected the military in the same way it has affected homes and banks — only the impact has been several orders of magnitude greater. Although technology now provides enormous capability, it does so at a great cost in terms of the logistics support we must now provide. Sophisticated weapons technology demands sophisticated support technology and a lot of it.

When a cave dweller's tribe battled another cave dweller's tribe, the weapons technology was simple — bare hands, perhaps a club, or maybe even a handy rock. Obviously, stones and clubs don't provide a great deal of combat capability, but they don't require much logistics support either. For the cave dweller, human endurance and skill, not weapon systems, were the primary factors determining success in battle.

Of course, weapons technology is not static. Stones and clubs gave way to knives and spears, and these gave way to bows and arrows. From a military perspective, bows and arrows not only provided more combat capability, they also required more logistics support. Various goods and services were needed, such as wood, string, feathers, flint, and the skills and tools required to fashion and use them properly.

Along with the amount of logistics needed to support technology, the importance of logistics also increased. Bow strings broke, and arrows were consumed. And in a bow and arrow war, those who ran short of a bow string or an arrow, particularly at some critical point in the conflict, probably lost both the battle and their lives.

The nature of warfare changed when the bow and arrow came

on the scene. It changed again when firearms first appeared. And it underwent a great transformation when the airplane was finally adopted as a military weapon. Indeed, conflicts speeded up with the introduction of each new military technology. More and more, the side with the better logistics – the ability to get goods and services rapidly in place – was the side that came out on top. This nation destroyed the Axis powers in World War II not so much with superior weaponry, but rather, by better logistics – by being able to overwhelm its opponents with a tidal wave of military goods and services.

In World War II, we had substantial, far-reaching logistics requirements. But we also had a thriving military industrial base to quickly provide the support we needed. We also enjoyed the buffering provided by vast oceans and large land masses, a buffering that gave us a great deal of time to get our act together.

Since then further advances in transportation, communication, and weapons technology have changed the environment even more, substantially making warfare a whole new ball game. On the positive side, these advances have given us far greater capability in the areas of reconnaissance, analysis, command and control, and target destruction. But on the negative side, they've also given our potential adversaries many of these same capabilities – and importantly, they've speeded up how fast things can happen.

The ultimate impact of modern military technology, as described in the preceding chapter, is the come-as-you-are war, which can start almost anywhere, easily threaten our most vital resources, occur with little or no notice, and grow to significant levels of intensity virtually overnight. Besides maintaining a strong nuclear deterrent force, the capability of fighting and winning a come-as-you-are conflict is really our biggest challenge today.

The Tail Wagging the Dog

Given the high-level technology we rely on so heavily and the come-as-you-are scenario we must plan for, what are the implications for logistics support? First, the tail will more and more wag the dog. In other words, logistics will increasingly become the single greatest factor in real combat capability. Second, we'd better find a way to cope with this reality, preferably by removing the need for logistics itself.

Over the years, we've become accustomed to thinking about logistics as something that follows everything else, something that reacts to operational needs. That's why we call it the logistics tail. When a medieval knight knew he was going into battle, he had arrows and bow strings prepared. Then, within a couple days, or perhaps a week, he was ready to go.

The same thing was basically true when we were dragged into World War II. After Pearl Harbor, the combat commanders tapped into the logistics system for airplanes, tanks, ships, and guns — and then waited 18 months or so until they had them before launching into any kind of major offensive. Like that medieval knight behind his castle's walls, we were still secure behind our oceans and land masses and still had time to further mobilize our defense industry and crank up our military might.

Because of present-day military technology, however, that approach is not going to work any more. One reason is the absolute dependency of our modern weapon systems on sophisticated logistics support. Another reason is the loss of sanctuary we've experienced because of the increased capability of our potential adversaries' weapons, coupled with the rapidity with which come-as-you-are conflicts can develop. Now we can't go to war without logistically supportable systems. And should a conflict develop, we can't hope to adequately support our systems fast enough or for a long enough time under the old reactive way of doing business.

It's important to realize that when defense experts talk about deploying, say, F-15s to a forward base, they're not just talking about deploying the airplanes. During World War II, deployment was relatively simple. The pilots could run out, climb into their aircraft, and head to the air patch nearest the fighting. Once there, they could keep their airplanes flying with baling wire and hometown garage know-how. But today, the technology of the F-15 has created the need for a great deal more support. Thus deployment includes supplying environmentally controlled, highly sophisticated avionics shops, war-readiness spares kits with thousands of items, complete replacement engines in modules, specialized ground-support equipment, elaborate inventory management systems, and large numbers of highly-skilled maintenance technicians.

Another important point is the criticality of many of the support items to the operation of the entire system. In many cases, not having some small bit part, perhaps one that only cost a few dollars, can effectively ground that $20 million F-15, taking it out of the fight. Considering what our weapon systems now cost, how relatively few we can afford to buy, and how long it takes to get them, the loss of even a single airplane through logistics shortfalls is an unconscionable act of waste.

So how do we deal with the problem? How do we cope with the great impediment to combat capability that logistics has become? Given the situation we're now in, given the technology we rely on, given the scenarios we must plan for – given all these things – costs, lead-times and supply pipelines must be our primary concern. Ultimately, logistics will be our primary limiting factor.

In practical terms, this reality poses a monumental problem. We must buy, produce, and stock the resources we'll need to fight and win, even in the face of uncertain and inadequate funding. And we must have many of these assets readily available, even prepositioned if possible, in some austere and often hostile parts of the world. But to maintain our combat capability, there is no other solution, because the fabric of weapon-system support is very delicate indeed. One tear, and the whole thing might well come undone.

For example, imagine a war that might develop in the Near East. Our rapid reaction force relies very heavily on our airlift capability to move weapons and support items to the theatre of conflict quickly. But unless we have control of the air, we certainly can't plan on having reliable airlift – and without the F-15s, we can't plan on having control of the air.

We've already talked about the F-15, and how complex and elaborate its logistics support is. What happens if something falls through the crack – if, say, we run short of fuel control valves or a particular circuit board for the fire-control system? Or what if we run out of consumables like fuel or munitions. Then we no longer have a squadron of F-15s — we have a squadron of static displays. But more importantly, we no longer have control of the air — which effectively means we no longer have airlift.

The end result, of course, is that the war is over, and we lose. We wouldn't have lost because we lacked the transports and bombers, or because we lacked guns and ammunition. We would have lost because we couldn't get the right supplies and services to those F-15s when and where needed.

That's why logistics is the critical factor in military operations today. To some extent, we can do without bombers, and to some extent, we can do without tanks and guns. But we can't risk doing without logistics, not to any extent. Logistics — like those spare parts we've heard so much about lately — is what really gives our weapon systems their capability and holds our whole defense capability together.

CHAPTER 6

Free Enterprise and Spare Parts

It's human nature to seek simple and neat solutions to complex problems. Such solutions are more readily conceptualized, they seem easier to manage, and they may even appear to require fewer resources. But very often our natural desire for an easy way out blinds us to the real challenge, thereby leading us to waste valuable time and resources working the wrong problem or only a part of the real problem. In the end, we often wind up making a bad situation even worse. In providing for our national security, the consequences could be ominous.

One of the most celebrated defense problems recently has been spare-parts overpricing, an issue that first surfaced in 1982. Since then, there has been widespread media coverage of such things as $1000 plastic stool caps and $30 screws. To some, spare-parts prices like these appear to be the result of mismanagement or corruption. In reality, however, they result from a set of interrelated factors. This is one of those very complex problems requiring not a simple and neat solution, but a well-thought-out and coherent set of solutions.

Combat Capability and the Spares Issue

To fully appreciate the significance of the spares issue, it's first necessary to understand how spares fit into the total defense picture. Our ability to deter an armed conflict and to fight and win should deterrence fail is directly related to our having the combat capability we need, along with the means of projecting it where it needs to be when it needs to be there – and then sustain it for as long as necessary. That's why national defense relies so heavily on logistics these days. And more and more, logistics relies on readiness and sustainability.

To achieve readiness and sustainability, spare parts must be available to the military. Recently, however, they have not been so easy to obtain. First, the military hasn't had the resources to buy the needed parts. Second, the military-industrial complex hasn't had the credibility in our society to compete successfully for these resources. Thus the spare-parts pricing issue has two distinct dimensions: affordability and credibility.

What Is a "Spare Part"?

Today, a spare part can be anything from a noncritical fastener costing a few cents to a radar processor costing tens of thousands of dollars. Yet virtually all of the overpricing cases touted in the media recently involved not high-value items like engines but low-value, low-visibility repair parts like washers and screws.

Of the 83,000 or so different items the Air Force buys each year, about 75 percent of the dollars go to purchasing 25 percent of the parts. Purchases of the big ticket items are very well audited, and controls are effective. These high visibility, budget line-items have not been part of the problem – and the lion's share of spares dollars have not really been involved in the whole pricing issue.

When considering the parts pricing problem, remember that spare parts are really not spare at all. The word *spares* brings to mind images of extraneous capability. For example, we carry a spare tire in our car on the outside chance that it might be needed, but more often than not, we'll never have occasion to use it. Or we'll have a spare bedroom in the house just in case somebody comes to visit, yet in no way would it be necessary for our day-to-day activities.

But given the nature of technology, and the effect it has in modern logistics, we just can't afford to think of spare parts in that way. There's nothing *spare* about military spare parts. We don't buy them on the chance that they may be needed. We buy them because we know they will be needed.

Imagine that you're going on a camping trip with a flashlight and spare batteries. Assuming your flashlight will burn for about 2 hours on a fresh set of batteries, and assuming you'll need about 4 hours of light, you decide to take at least one set of "spare" batteries. But they're not really spare in the true sense of the word. They're not extra – they're absolutely essential. You know for a fact that if you use the light, you'll need the batteries. You also know that if you don't have the spares when the batteries go dead, it doesn't matter how bright your flashlight is designed to be. And if you don't have the spares when the batteries go dead, not only will your investment in the flashlight be wasted, but the original need that prompted you to buy the flashlight will not be met.

The same thing is basically true of the military services' inventory. Today, in this era of high technology, very little can be accomplished unless the equipment in our weapon systems is functioning. If you are driving your car across the Mojave Desert in August, such seemingly minor and inexpensive parts as the fan belt, fuel line filter, or radiator hoses are not so minor if they break unexpectedly. This is even more true for modern weapon systems, because we're depending on state-of-the-art technology.

Fortunately, the breakdowns in our weapon systems are not unexpected. For the most part, we know when such failures are going to happen. By collecting and analyzing data, we can precisely predict when parts will break, just as surely as we can predict when flashlight batteries will go dead. And we know the lead times required to purchase replacements. These predictions are the basis for buying, stocking, and distributing these so-called spare parts.

When considering the spare parts pricing issue, keep things in perspective. Remember that thinking of spares as extraneous is misleading. They're actually the low-value, bit-part essentials that we know will wear out or break. We know in advance that our systems will need them in order to do the job they were designed and purchased to do.

The Complexity of the Overpricing Issue

Without doubt, Americans have both the right and duty to demand a full return on their tax dollars, especially those used for national defense. And without doubt, revelations about $1000 plastic stool caps or $30 machine screws have properly raised serious questions about the management capabilities, if not the integrity, of our military-industrial complex. Unfortunately, the indictment of spare-parts pricing not only demonstrates waste, which by itself is bad enough, but it also hurts the credibility of vital defense programs and effectively decreases our ability to buy the protection this country requires.

To take effective action — the kind that would provide a better return on the taxpayer's dollar and help restore confidence in the military-industrial complex — it is first necessary to identify and understand the many causes of the problem and their relationship to one another.

The spares problem has a host of causes, all stemming from the government's inability, for a number of reasons, to fully exploit the strengths of our free-enterprise economy. For example, during many critical years there was substantial economic inflation in our country, especially in the aerospace industry. Then there was the *decade of neglect* — years of gross underfunding for defense with the attendant withering of much of our industrial base and the loss of many skilled and experienced professionals in government service. Partly because of lower funding during this time, the military had to buy in smaller quantities, which violated a cardinal rule of free-enterprise economics. Then it had to pay the high price associated with modern military technology, while bearing the high cost of carry-over technologies to keep older systems operating. Finally, the armed forces had to deal with vastly increased requirements, many of them unplanned, and most of them needing immediate attention to maintain our national security.

There's no need to dwell on the inflation experienced in this nation during the '70s. Suffice it to say that in 1970, a family with an income of $10,000 per year had $8640 to spend after paying federal income and social security taxes. Ten years later, at the time we were rapidly buying defense products to make up for past neglect, that same family needed a gross income of $20,187 to have the same spending power. Most of that increase represented the generally high inflation rates of the mid- and late-'70s.

In the aerospace industry, however, the inflation rate went even higher, driven by the need for high-demand skills, exotic materials, and expensive retooling. A 1983 report by the Joint Senior Services Review Team found that in 1980 alone, the producer-price index, weighted for the labor and raw materials needed to produce high-performance jet-engine parts, ran well over 26 percent.

The inflation factor becomes even more significant when one considers how the federal cataloging system tended to carry over prices from one year to another. Very often, when a particular item was not purchased for a while, the catalog continued to show the price at last purchase, perhaps a figure that had been carried over for 10 years or so and that thus had little relevance to modern economic realities. That's like finding a 10-year-old Sears catalog in the attic, putting in an order, and then receiving a bill at today's prices.

Another factor to consider is the role that the neglect of the '70s played in driving up prices in the '80s. The serious underfunding of defense during that period (see Figure 6) led to our buying rubber on the ramp at the expense of spare parts. Our government made conscious decisions to modernize the force — to spend the limited money available for new systems instead of support.

By FY 76, the Air Force was buying only 37 percent of the spare parts it required. By FY 80, spares funding had fallen to only 24 percent of the requirement. Considering the new weapon systems coming on board and the absolutely essential nature of spares, we were setting ourselves up for a serious spare parts deficiency. It came back to haunt us in the 1980s.

During this decade of neglect, the military couldn't buy as many new systems as it needed either. So old systems were modified to give them new capabilities. But that approach had the effect of aging the inventory — and therefore increased the need for spare parts, further exacerbating the spares deficiency.

All these problems wouldn't have been so serious if the industrial base had remained healthy, and the many spare-parts

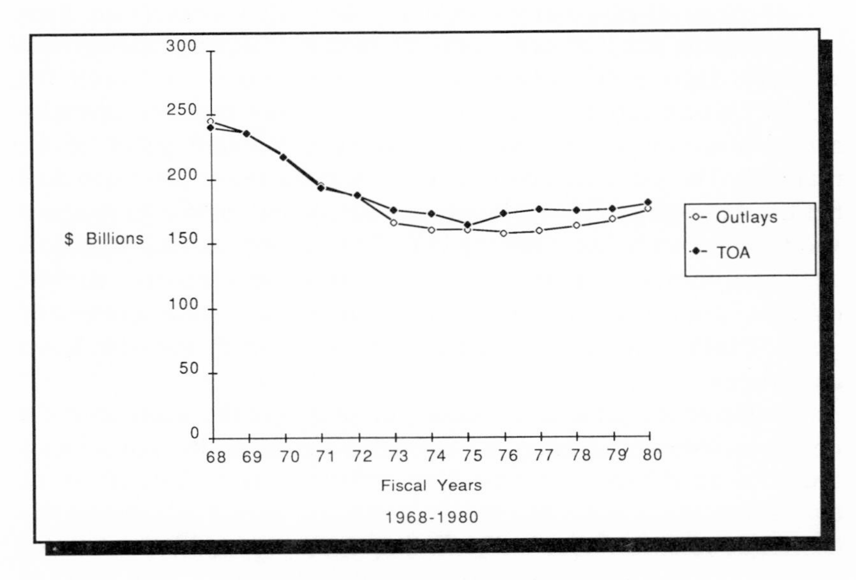

Fig. 6. The Decade of Neglect

(Data from "Defense Total Obligation Authority and Outlays 1964-1983," Report of the Secretary of Defense to the Congress on the FY 1984 Budget, FY 1985 Authorization Request and FY 1984-88 Defense Programs, *Washington, D.C.: U.S. Government Printing Office, Feb. 1, 1983, p. 63.)*

suppliers had remained on line to compete for contracts. But budget cuts of the '70s also decimated America's defense industry. Almost half our defense suppliers, with all their experience and expertise, simply vanished during those years. The number of aerospace suppliers alone dropped almost 42 percent, from 6000 in 1967 to a little over 3000 by the 1980s. Thus, at the time demand was peaking, the means of supply were withering.

Another aspect of the loss of contractors was the attendant loss of skilled defense workers. In the private sector many experienced people were forced from defense-related jobs as defense contracts declined. The defense industry experienced shortfalls of 33 percent for engineers, 49 percent for computer specialists, and 84 percent for statisticians.

In government, many skilled and dedicated workers involved in negotiating procurement contracts and monitoring pricing were laid off. During the 1970s, the Air Force Logistics Command (AFLC) alone suffered a 31 percent reduction in civilian personnel, professionals with hard-to-find expertise and years of experience. The personnel cuts at AFLC left far fewer people to do a rapidly expanding job. And without the skilled people to monitor all the contracting and pricing AFLC was involved in, it became necessary to focus efforts on the higher price items like turbine blades – neglecting, to some extent, the bit parts like screws and bolts. That's why the pricing problem was limited to these lower value items.

Another by-product of underfunding was the need to make smaller military purchases. Buying more things tends to make each one of them cheaper, whether it be apples by the bag or oil by the barrel. But that's not how defense purchases were made during this time. In some cases, like a family on a tight budget, the military couldn't afford large quantities of some items. Also, with evolving technology so quickly outdating equipment, the military couldn't run the risk of investing in large numbers of items, especially when the weapon system inventory was being reduced, and modifications were coming down the road on many of the systems remaining.

Rapidly expanding technology also forced prices up in many other ways – especially in an environment where competition for scarce resources was keen, and suppliers were few. For example, that $30 machine screw for the F-4 fighter airplane was not just a run-of-the-mill, galvanized steel fastener – not with the heat resistance, precision, and hardness required by its high technology application. Although we paid too much for many common-use items, this screw wasn't one of them. The Air Force simply couldn't buy titanium and tungsten machine screws in the local hardware store for a buck a bag. Rather, they had to be machined in a specialized, highly technical process – and, in this particular case, they had to be made of some scarce materials. And that costs money.

But the problem is even more complex, because along with paying the high costs of procuring and working with strategic materials like titanium, we had to deal at the same time in a less competitive marketplace. With fewer defense contractors available and increasing demands for technical sophistication and scarce materials, the military was forced to do business with fewer companies. As a result, the Air Force spent only about 20 percent of its procurement dollars competitively in 1982.

This competition problem was made even worse by the proprietary rights many contractors maintained over their data, as well as the urgent need we had for the parts themselves. Suddenly, after the invasion of Afghanistan and the seizing of our embassy in Iran in the late '70s, we realized that the world was not such a nice place after all. In fact, the situation was not unlike having a new computer-controlled, fuel-injected car break down in the middle of nowhere, and having to buy the one critical part from the only mechanic around.

Although new technology certainly contributed to driving up the cost of defense, old technology also played a major role. For example, anyone who tries to maintain a 5-tube AM radio from the '60s will find that replacing just a single tube today will cost more than the entire radio cost originally. The reason, of course, is that tube technology has largely been supplanted by solid-state technology. And that's why most people have thrown away their 5-tube radios.

There was a day when, figuratively, the military also threw away its 5-tube radios — that time during the early postwar era when we built thousands of new weapon systems and then discarded and replaced them when they became unreliable and outdated. For example, we built 2000 B-47s — then a few years later, when B-47 technology became outdated, we sent them all to the bone yard and built more than 800 B-52s to replace them.

But we haven't thrown away those B-52s, even though they're almost three decades old. Given budget restraints in past years, it's just been too expensive to replace them. And the B-52 is not alone. Today the average Air Force aircraft is about 16 years old, not counting Guard and Reserve systems, which are even older.

There are fewer and fewer contractors around to support these aging systems. This lack of competition drives up the costs of spare parts for older technology, because few companies want to produce outdated technology anymore. There's no future in it, and fewer people are trained or are willing to be trained to do it. How many electrical engineers coming out of college today even take a single course in vacuum tube theory?

The Costs of Catching Up

Beginning in 1980, there was great pressure on all the services to overcome the deficiencies that accumulated during the '70s. Yet the industrial base was thin, competition had waned, resources for new technology were in great demand, and much of our weapon system technology had grown old and difficult to support.

There just wasn't time to recover in an economically sound way. Responding to the need for increased security, military outlays in constant dollars suddenly rose as fast as they had fallen 10 years earlier. The emphasis was on buying whatever was needed to defend this nation – at whatever the cost.

Thus, such procurement mechanisms as the fixed-price redeterminable contract were instituted to ensure, in advance, that the military would get what limited production capability would be needed when it became available. The military had to commit itself to future buys, without knowing what the exact price would be.

In effect, prior neglect coupled with a deteriorating international situation forced us to play the futures market in defense. As anyone who plays the futures market knows, doing so is a risky business. The military took the risk, and in terms of maintaining our national security, we all won. But in terms of saving dollars, we lost. With the upward pressures resulting from inflation, the forces of supply and demand, and the intricacies of the technologies we were supporting, prices went up too. And so did the cost of defense.

The point is that the parts-pricing problem was not a simple case of mismanagement or corruption as many believed it to be. Simple solutions, like threatening criminal prosecution of corporate executives, obviously would not redress the causes of the problem or prevent it from occurring again. Threatening to throw someone in jail wouldn't keep worldwide inflation rates down, it wouldn't make old technology any easier to support, and it wouldn't reverse years of neglecting defense concerns. But it would cause hard feelings, intensify the adversarial relationship between the military and the private sector, impair communication, and in the end waste precious resources and harm the defense effort.

Although individual elements of the problem, like the shortage of procurement specialists, could have been solved effectively in isolation (for example, by hiring more people), the overall problems of cost and defense industry credibility had to be attacked on many fronts.

Ensuring Affordability and Credibility

In searching for effective solutions to the complex issues at hand, the Department of Defense (DOD) moved to better exploit the strengths of our free enterprise system, our society's great inherent strength. The steps DOD took to control costs and improve credibility involved not constraints and needless regulation but rather free competition and better integration through improved communication and understanding.

DOD efforts began after the Hancock Report, put together by AFLC's Oklahoma City Air Logistics Center, first surfaced in the fall of 1982. It brought to light what appeared to be wasteful expenditures on low-value items. This was followed up by internal AFLC audits, a Government Accounting Office investigation, and many other federal inquiries. Several initiatives were then generated to begin dealing with the problem.

For example, AFLC set up a Pacer Price program in the spring of '83 with the goal of determining what low-value items should cost. These target prices could then be used as a bargaining tool by government procurement officers negotiating contracts. There was also a movement to revitalize the Air Force's Zero Overpricing program, so that those requisitioning items from the supply system would have the means of challenging the prices they were charged.

The Air Force Management Analysis Group (AFMAG) also conducted an investigation and issued a final report in early fall 1983. The AFMAG put sufficient emphasis on the pricing issue to move Pacer Price from ad hoc status to a formal activity under the newly formed Office of the Competition Advocate, which underscored the commitment to pay more attention to the procurement process. As a result, the Air Force began handling more low-value items in much the same way that it had been successfully dealing with high-value spares. Additionally, the Air Force intensified its efforts to encourage more competition — letting free enterprise, wherever possible, naturally control the cost of defense. AFLC also made much progress in getting the extra staff required to effectively manage these new programs. Other actions were taken to better integrate military needs with the private sector: there was improved communications with the private sector, including numerous meetings with industry, and the bid rooms in the air logistics centers were upgraded in order to better get the word out about defense requirements.

Not Doing Anything Dumb

Although the major thrust in instituting these reforms was to achieve cost savings and increase credibility, there was great concern about not doing anything dumb. The military had to make sure that it did not compromise quality and that what it bought would meet the test. Even a bit part costing a few dollars can bring down an entire weapon system if that part can't perform its function.

Also, care had to be taken not to destroy the health of the defense industry in the process of getting a better handle on costs. Creating a cutthroat environment within the defense industry could eventually weaken everyone. That's something the military could not risk, not when the security of this nation rests directly on the shoulders of private enterprise. To shortsightedly limit the rewards that should rightfully go hand-in-hand with that enterprise would be tantamount to tearing down the wall of achievement that has protected our society for so long.

For years, America's defense industry has made the substantial capital investments necessary to produce the weapon systems we've needed. It has created and nurtured the necessary skills, and it has expanded its corporate memory of how to get things done. As the military continues to seek cost savings, it must take fully into account the long-term impact of its actions. In the defense business, to throw the baby out with the bath water would represent not only great injustice and great waste—it would also threaten the existence of our democratic society.

CHAPTER 7

The Leverage of Reliability

We often become so preoccupied with solving an unsolvable problem that we blind ourselves to another approach — one which would eliminate the problem altogether. Thus, we expend more resources than we need for less return than we want and very often at precisely the time we can least afford to do so.

For example, consider the cherry picking industry in Michigan. For many years, cherry growers had to deal with an unsolvable problem: the daytime heat often spoiled the picked cherries before they could be properly stored. To cope with the problem as best they could, growers used large numbers of people to harvest and store the cherries at a feverish pace.

Then someone tried a new approach. Generators and lights were brought into the orchards so the cherries could be picked during the early morning hours before the sun came up. Relatively few pickers could then produce a larger, unspoiled harvest while working at a normal pace. As it turned out, the cost of generators and lights, when amortized over their expected life, was less than the cost of the extra manpower required for daytime picking. And, of course, with nighttime picking, the spoilage problem simply went away.

Why talk about cherry picking in a book on the military and national defense? The point is that logistics is to military operations what hot weather is to the cherry picking industry. Logistics is the single greatest impediment to having enough combat capability today, especially since the resources available to solve the logistics problem (money, time, skills, and material) are inadequate. Furthermore, the situation is not likely to improve in the future — at least not given our current mode of thinking.

When faced with its "unsolvable" problem, the cherry-picking industry effectively did away with it with new thinking. But can we do the same thing for logistics – can we eliminate the logistics problem altogether with a new approach? Is there a practical way for the armed forces to have the capability of fulfilling all of their military commitments, anywhere in the world and at any time, and in the process save billions of dollars annually? Those dollars could then be used to address the deficiencies that might still exist in our defense programs and to do other things that would make our economy even stronger.

There is a way we can do this and that's to do away with the requirement for support: We can build weapon systems that can accomplish their wartime tasks without the need for spare parts, engines, and sophisticated maintenance. That alone would eliminate the logistics problem – and in the process, remove from our shoulders an awesome resource burden.

This proposal is not some mindless fantasy, nor is it a pie-in-the-sky idea. Purely and simply, it's better system reliability – and it's available now.

The Acceptance of Unreliability

Many have charged that we're a use-and-replace society – and not without some justification. Studies show that only 5 to 15 percent of what the average American throws away on any particular day could truly be classified as garbage. Indeed, much of what we throw away is either stuff that is broken or stuff that we know from experience will be broken if we use it much longer.

This attitude has been many years in the making. As far back as the Industrial Revolution, our machines were unreliable. But that's because progress is inevitable – and even when technology is crude, if it responds to a real need, it will be used. For example, during the 1800s, we invented incandescent bulbs to light our way, pneumatic tires to carry heavy loads, and the telegraph to better communicate with our own kind. But those bulbs often burned out in a matter of hours, pneumatic tire tubes were notorious for bursting on bumpy roads, and telegraph lines were frequently down. But we accepted such unreliable machines in those days, because we couldn't build them any better. Just to build some of them at all pushed hard at the outer limits of our capability.

One need only look back at the early automobile for a prime example of unreliable technology. In those days, people who didn't know how to make mechanical repairs didn't drive alone. It was a rare outing, indeed, when a hose didn't break, a radiator didn't boil over, or a tire didn't go flat. And although many of the old engines turned out to be surprisingly durable, a person who kept a car for any length of time could plan on burned-out clutches, failed magnetos, and broken fan belts.

Automobiles today, of course, are more reliable in many respects, although they still leave a great deal to be desired — especially considering how far we've moved up on the learning curve for much of the technology we're using. Just look at the new car recalls issued by manufacturers each year for problems in fuel, electrical, and cooling systems. These defects do not occur because we don't fully understand carburetion, current flow, or thermodynamics. They occur because we haven't tried hard enough to design breakdowns out by designing reliability in.

A quick look at predicted automobile repair data for the past 5 years or so would demonstrate a striking dichotomy between the reliability of virtually all the cars designed and built in this country and the reliability of those designed and built by certain foreign competitors. The problem is not that reliability can't be achieved at competitive prices — the problem is that we just haven't been doing it, even though not doing so has made absolutely no sense at all.

The costs of automotive unreliability in this country today are staggering — and not just in terms of jobs and prestige lost to foreign competition. Department of Transportation statistics show that a typical American car kept for 100,000 miles or so will probably need a new water pump, alternator, brake pads, starter, fuel pump, catalytic converter, and lower ball joints — and require substantial work on the transmission and carburetor or fuel injection system.

With energy costs as high as they are, Americans still only spend about six and a half billion dollars on gas and oil. But they spend a whopping $26 billion on auto repairs. Such is the dollar cost of automotive unreliability. And remember, this doesn't take into consideration other costs of having a car break down – the costs of inconvenience, lost opportunities, work missed, vacations ruined, and even lives endangered.

Why have we allowed this to happen? The answer is that, over a period of time, we came to accept a standard of unreliability in cars and developed corresponding mind-sets. Until recently, most Americans traded for a new car every few years because not doing so was considered to be asking for trouble. And at the time, prices and interest rates were low enough to make frequent trading an easy, workable solution to what had become the given of unreliability.

Like Americans and their cars, the military has somehow come to accept the lack of reliability as an inherent feature of high-technology weapon systems. Yet like carburetor problems and car electrical system failures, the causes of weapon system unreliability aren't a mystery. We know precisely what causes parts to break, we can predict precisely when failures will occur, and more importantly, we already have the know-how and capability to design and build them so that they will not break – at least not nearly so often.

The reason we haven't embraced reliability is that we've trained ourselves not to think about unreliability or acknowledge the impact it has both in terms of combat capability and dollars. Like so many American car buyers today, we accept the fact that our military machines will break and that such failures are simply the inevitable price we must pay for our reliance on sophisticated technology.

That mind-set, more than anything else, is responsible for our designing and building systems to go fast and high but not reliably for any length of time. That mind-set is responsible not only for the degradations we're now seeing in weapon system readiness and sustainability but also for the increased allocations of defense dollars we're faced with just to keep these systems going.

Reliability and Military Capability

Present day military strategy and tactics are built around the power of modern military technology. It follows, therefore, that to the extent the necessary technology can't be supported, our strategy and tactics must be called into question. That's why the true measure of merit for our weapon systems today is not whether they look good on the ramp, not how high or how fast they can fly, but how reliably they can do the wartime mission they're tasked to do.

When we talk about the military's reliance on high technology, we're really talking about its reliance on certain critical subsystems. In the modern military environment, all of these critical systems must be functioning at nearly 100 percent reliability if we're to have any real assurance that our weapon systems will be effective in war.

Here's one example from the Air Force. To determine the probability of a particular weapon system's being effective in the wartime scenario, the Air Force has to look at several indicators. The context, of course, is the mission – and in the case of many front-line combat aircraft, system effectiveness equates to the destruction of an enemy target, or what the military calls damage expectancy.

To determine effectiveness (damage expectancy) for a particular weapon system employed under a particular war plan, four factors are considered: launch success, weapon system reliability, probability of penetration, and probability of kill. For a typical system, it is not unusual to find both the probabilities of launch success and target penetration to be up around the 98th percentile – meaning these warplanes are all but certain to get off the ground and reach their targets. And if that's all a sortie required, every mission would be a success. But two other factors must be considered: probability of kill and system reliability.

At one time, the probability of destroying a target was significantly lessened by the munitions employed. Bombs were often released at high altitude, and followed a long, natural glide path through unpredictable winds. They often missed their target altogether. Today, however, the military has *preferred munitions,* like state-of-the-art missiles and smart bombs, which are precisely guided to the target. These alone can vastly improve the likelihood of hitting what's aimed at. Indeed, it is not unusual for a single airplane today employing preferred munitions to have the same probability of destroying the target as several warplanes using older, more traditional ordnance. The advantages of state-of-the-art munitions are so great that what was once a serious limiting factor is no longer a significant consideration – at least not when preferred munitions are employed.

What this means is this: in terms of being able to accomplish the wartime mission, three of the four factors determining weapon system effectiveness have been dealt with successfully. But what about that one remaining factor, reliability? How much would the lack of reliability degrade system effectiveness in the typical wartime scenario? To figure that, we have to look at the reliability of each system critical to the mission in terms of the length of the mission sortie – or, in other words, look at the chances that all the critical systems will function reliably for the entire duration of the mission.

For example, consider the aviation-electronics (avionics) bomb-navigation (bomb-nav) system that allows a modern warplane to precisely locate and attack a target. Say that such a system had a mean time between failure (MTBF) of 2 hours on an aircraft tasked to do a 6-hour, high-precision bombing mission. If that were the case, it really wouldn't matter if the aircraft launched and penetrated the enemy's defenses successfully, or if it carried smart bombs. The warplane's ability to do the job would be compromised as soon as this bomb-nav system failed, which it would do on the average of every two hours. This one part of the avionics system, would, in and of itself, be the limiting factor. And remember, the way things are today, all the other systems on board probably would not be 100 percent reliable either. Consequently, the reliability of that weapon system on this mission would be no better (and probably worse) than the reliability of its bomb-nav system. Because to do the job, all of the critical systems must function properly for the duration of the mission.

System reliability is the single most significant limiting factor we must deal with today – not launch success, probability of penetration, or probability of kill. Dealing with unreliability today requires that the Air Force plan to send more planes than would otherwise be necessary to accomplish a particular mission. And this translates into a greater need for expensive weapon systems, highly skilled people — and the increased risk of combat losses.

Given existing levels of reliability, what does it take to have the combat capability we need? It takes extra weapon systems ready to go whenever and wherever needed. It takes extra preferred munitions available whenever and wherever needed. And it takes additional flight crews, skilled technicians, sophisticated maintenance facilities, war-readiness kits, replacement engines, and other required support ready to go whenever and wherever needed.

These days — considering how fast conflicts may develop, how spread out our vital interests are, how long we have neglected the problem, and how vast our shortages in support are — we have some very serious needs to be considered. The single greatest limitation to our having the combat capability we need today is logistics, the single greatest impediment to our having the kind of logistically supportable systems we must have is the lack of system reliability, and our greatest leverage in generating combat capability is in the area of reliability improvement.

Reducing System Failure Rates

To achieve the effectiveness our force really should have, we'd only need a modest increase in the average time our systems could operate without a significant failure. If we could build weapon systems that would not fail on the average for 1300 hours or so, we would have the reliability we'd need to efficiently and effectively accomplish the wartime tasking. That increase in reliability would substantially reduce the probability of our suffering combat losses — and would greatly enhance the deterrent value of our forces.

The technology to achieve this kind of reliability has already been substantially bought and paid for, and we've already built highly complex systems with at least that level of reliability. The Navy has a navigation system on the F-14 fighter plane with a 2000 hour mean time between failure (MTBF). The Air Force has a signal processor for the F-15 with a predicted MTBF of 10,000 hours. And the new ring laser gyro is expected to run for an average 40,000 hours without a failure.

Of course, the ideal is a totally reliable weapon system, one which would need virtually no logistics support except for consumables like fuel and munitions. Think of the enormous, almost incalculable benefits that would accrue from such reliability. Think, for example, how much more effective our existing first-line fighters would be if they could be deployed without the need for specialized maintenance capabilities, war-readiness kits, replacement engines, and the multitude of other support items. And think about how much more secure the free world would be.

The up-front cost of achieving this kind of reliability would be high, but it might not be as high as some think. And without doubt, the return in future cost savings alone would be considerable, especially given the fact that we now keep our weapon systems for 20 to 30 years. Imagine the cost savings in maintenance and the potential savings in reduced airlift requirements, in everything from number of transports to flying hours – and imagine what it would mean if we didn't have to recruit, train, and deploy as many maintenance technicians.

We would benefit across the board. We wouldn't need all those facilities, all that equipment, or all that material. Many of the highly sophisticated, highly expensive maintenance shops would become a thing of the past – and a good part of the entire military supply system could simply go away.

The budget figures for Air Force Logistics Command show just how expensive it is for the Air Force alone to support its present force structure. The breakout depicted in Figure 7, and the precise figures in Table 2, indicate just how fertile an area for cost savings reliability improvements represent. For example, what if we did away with aircraft and missile spare parts and eliminated those modifications required just to maintain designed capability? And what if we reduced support equipment by 75 percent? These alone would have decreased the FY 85 budget by almost $8¼ billion.

Additional savings in operations and maintenance costs would have amounted to about $9½ billion. These savings, when coupled with other savings in civilian logistics personnel, could easily free up 20 percent of the entire Air Force budget to be used in more productive and meaningful ways.

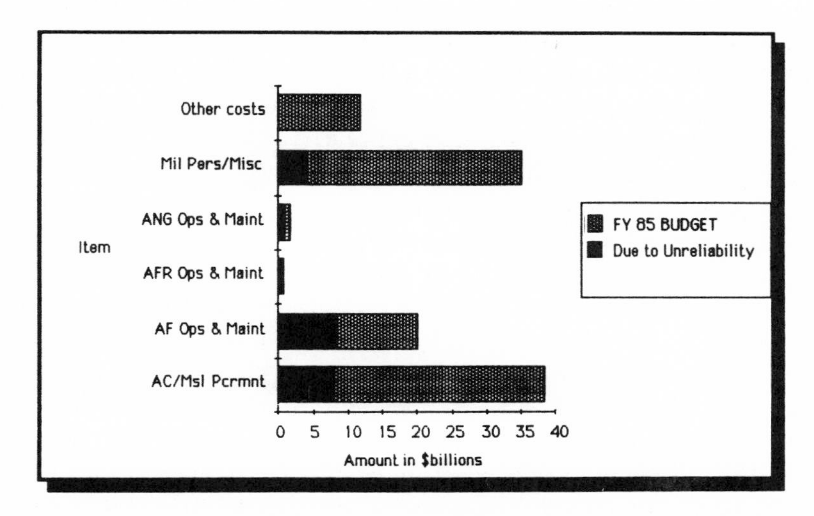

Fig. 7. Fiscal Year 1985 Air Force Budget: The Cost of Unreliability. *(Data from "Cost Associated with Item Failure," Headquarters AFLC/XRS, Tab 1: Air Force Accounting and Finance Center/CWML, "Analysis of FY 85 Presidents Budget," March 8, 1984, unpublished.)*

Table 2. Fiscal Year 1985 Air Force Budget: The Cost of Unreliability

Item	Amount $billions
Aircraft/Missile Procurement	38.498
(Mods/Spares/75% Support Equip)	8.262
Air Force Operations & Maintenance	20.235
(Repair/Modifications)	8.344
Air Force Reserve Ops & Maintenance	.883
(Repair/Modifications)	.562
Air National Guard Ops & Maintenance	1.862
(Repair/Modifications)	.806
Military Personnel/Misc Funding	35.354
(AFLC/Base Maintenance Personnel)	4.281
Other Costs	11.898
TOTAL APPROPRIATIONS	**108.730**
(Amount due to Unreliability)	**22.555**

(Data from "Cost Associated with Item Failure," Headquarters AFLC/XRS, Tab 1: Air Force Accounting and Finance Center/CWML, "Analysis of FY 85 Presidents Budget," March 8, 1984, unpublished.)

Over a 30-year period (a typical weapon-system life cycle), assuming a 5 percent inflation rate, the savings would amount to $1238 billion – which is almost enough to retire the national debt. And this is a very conservative estimate. It doesn't take into account the costs of military personnel, construction, research, development, test, evaluation, and the wide spectrum of miscellaneous procurement expenses resulting from the fact that our weapon systems are unreliable.

However, these figures do assume almost totally reliable systems. Although total reliability is possible and no doubt inevitable in the future, it is certainly not in the cards in the near term. But smaller improvements in reliability are achievable now – and even these more modest gains would have a significant impact on defense spending.

If you were to look at a composite of our fighter aircraft, and model, say, their spares requirements against MTBF, this is what you'd find: for a 25 percent improvement in MTBF, perhaps from 500 hours to 625 hours, you could reduce the spares requirement almost 40 percent and still maintain the same aircraft availability. And if you could double the present MTBF, you would eliminate almost 80 percent of the present spares requirement. Figure 8 shows how increasing MTBF (that is, raising reliability) for various aircraft types would affect the need for spares.

Think about that – think about the incredible savings in dollars this would lead to – think about how much more affordable our national defense would be – think about how much more prepared we would be to defend our vital interests anywhere in the world – think about the enhanced deterrent value our forces would have – and think about this: much of this improvement in MTBF is well within the realm of possibility. The same technology that allows us to maintain missiles on alert with verifiable reliability or blast satellites into a very stressful environment with no failures and no need for calibration is there waiting for us now. We need only step up to the problem, pay the investment costs up front, and take advantage of that great leverage increased reliability can give us.

It makes so much sense that we do so that in time such changes are inevitable. Because the lack of system reliability so

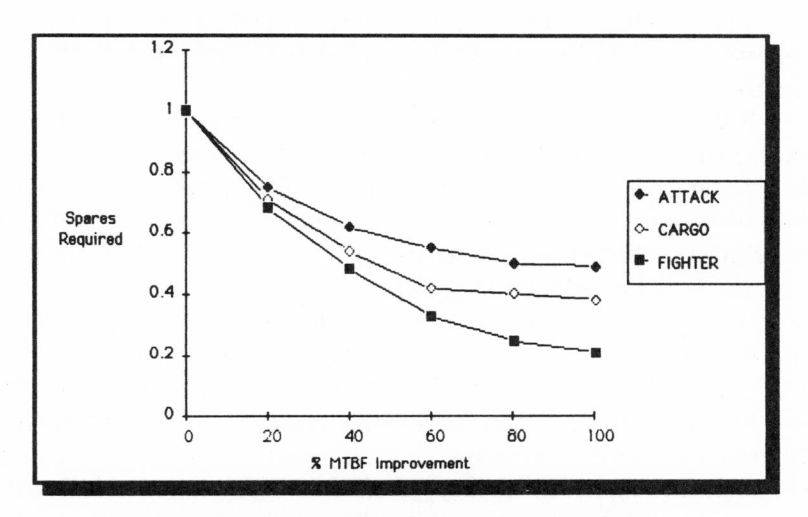

Fig. 8. Composite Spares Required *vs* MTBF.
(Data from "Cost Associated with Item Failures," Headquarters AFLC/XRS, Tab 2: "MTBF Impact Study (BP15 Peacetime Spares)," March 8, 1984, unpublished.)

grievously drains our national resources, burdens our economy, and limits our military security, we'll have to build more reliable systems. Doing so will ultimately go a long way toward balancing the federal budget, an effort that will continue to take on increased importance in the years ahead.

Historically, whenever serious problems have existed and the technology has become available to solve them, people have in time naturally exploited this technology to solve those problems. The chief concern now, however, is that, considering the dangers we face and the vulnerabilities we have, we may not have time to let nature take its course.

Where Babies Come From

One way to solve our current reliability problem is to go back to where weapon system babies are born. If the military can require reliability up front in the specifications for its new weapon systems, it will ultimately achieve reliability on the ramp where it counts.

Because of the way our system works today, reliability has tended to be an afterthought. Until recently we've paid little attention to the funding and procurement of more reliable weapons. And we've never really tried to make an effort to achieve the kind of reliability necessary for weapons to do their wartime tasking without considerable logistics support.

A large part of the problem is inherent in the requirements process, which determines how many of which weapon will be needed. Partly, it grows out of the free-enterprise defense industry and the profit motive that drives this industry. Certainly profit is not bad. Quite the contrary, it's our economy's great strength. Throughout American history, profit has been responsible for the innovation and Yankee ingenuity that have served us so well for over 200 years.

But the profit motive in private industry affects the military requirements process. It influences what we buy and it reinforces our infatuation with procuring more and more weapon systems at the expense of the supportability these systems must have to be effective in time of war.

For years now the military has been trading off real combat capability for the illusion of capability, an illusion of total numbers in an inventory, not of real capability like sorties that can be flown or ordnance that can be delivered. For example, in the past if the Air Force purchased, say, 100 new airplanes, it expected only 75 of them to be operational when needed. What's worse, even those expectations were optimistic. What the Air Force typically wound up with was only 50 airplanes that could actually go to war or even meet our peacetime operational and training requirements.

To achieve the reliability we need, private enterprise must take the lead, because the requirements the military responds to when it buys new systems don't just come from the military. To a considerable extent, these requirements come to the military from the defense industry via marketing and proposal strategies. Many times, in order to allow enough lead time for development, the prime contractor will have already begun independent research and development (IR&D). In effect, the contractor has already often determined what it wants to produce before the formal acquisition process begins.

The initial IR&D is an evaluation of current and future technology along with a preliminary assessment of the operational environment and resultant service needs. It is the preconceptual phase of weapon system development, and it is heavily dependent on existing technology.

It's important to recognize that system design actually begins in this preconceptual phase. The contractor validates the design through the process of marketing it to one of the services. If successful, the contractor gets a contract. Thus, to a substantial degree, the weapon capabilities devised by contractors create military requirements. In the defense business, then, the prime contractors are where babies really come from.

The point is that it's not until after the prime contractor completes the preconceptual, IR&D assessment that he'll even begin discussions with the military. It's not until the demonstration/validation phase that a system program office (SPO) and deputy program manager for logistics (DPML) will be assigned. The logistics people get together with the contractor, but only to plan and implement a support strategy.

From a logistics viewpoint — and consequently from a combat capability viewpoint — this sequence of events poses a serious problem. For one thing, under the current scheme, system design clearly precedes support design, and support design is where reliability concerns would normally surface. Consequently, by the time support strategies are formulated, they generally must react to what usually is an already unreliable system design. Thus, the lack of reliability is normally locked in from the start.

A big part of the problem, of course, is the mind-sets that the military services have when looking at new system requirements. Typically, the military has seen new systems in terms of the enhanced operational capability they will provide: how much faster or higher they will go. The military has also tended to be very specific about such operational parameters as mach number, altitude and G-loads. Logistics factors, however, until recently have received no such attention — not from the military and certainly not from the prime contractor. In terms of reliability, there's been little effort made by any of the services to identify the war plan tasking, to formulate reliability requirements against that tasking, and to include these requirements in its design specifications.

Rarely are operational and support requirements fused into a cohesive whole. And rarely is there any motivation in the process for a prime contractor to trade off operational parameters, which the military has looked for specifically, for enhanced supportability and reliability, which it traditionally has tended to gloss over or totally ignore. That's why the incentive has always been for a prime contractor to produce, say, tight high-performance engines rather than lower-thrust, more durable ones.

Getting Priorities Straight

The existing acquisition process isn't all bad — indeed, it's mostly good. It's free enterprise — what this country is all about, and what has made it a great nation, economically. But the military must learn to be a more effective player in this process, given the changes in the environment and the challenges we face. And the first thing the military must do is exert more influence, up front, in the development of weapon system designs. And that means getting its act together at the conception of a new system, with the contractor's independent research and development efforts.

Contractors slant their IR&D towards technologies and design approaches that they are comfortable with. In effect, they design for resources they have access to and control over. Each prime contractor has in-house design and production capabilities that have evolved over time in response to corporate strategies. These capabilities, of course, significantly affect the way each contractor sees the world. Thus, they affect the requirements the contractor will generate, and consequently, the weapon system and support packages the military will ultimately buy.

The prime contractors' mind-sets and methodologies will not

be easy to change. Not only will the economics of the process impede change, but also the sheer inertia of the whole system will tend to resist our efforts.

The military, of course, is an important part of the weapons acquisition process and must bear its share of responsibility for the problems we're facing. For years now, as a customer for the prime contractors, it has placed major emphasis on operational performance. The result was often adoption of immature technologies that are unreliable and difficult to support. The military has also been guilty of taking the short-term approach to defining basic requirements, necessitating constant system changes.

Those responsible for providing logistics support can also take some of the blame. They haven't always done a good job of articulating their requirements, often coming up with second-thought or after-the-fact needs. And those responsible for developing systems have frequently become bogged down in day-to-day activities, failing to do an adequate job of balancing system parameters with long-term, life-cycle implications.

But progress has been made. The military services, certainly the Air Force, have come a long way in developing new processes, paying more attention to such concerns as life-cycle costs, and creating greater incentives for increased reliability. But the surface has just been scratched, we still have a long way to go, and we may not have much time to get there.

The key to doing what we need to do is to take advantage of the innovative strengths of free enterprise. We must make needed change worthwhile financially to the prime contractor, the one who usually establishes the requirements in the first place. We must find some way to motivate defense contractors to think more in terms of system reliability. That means that the military, as the user and customer, must place as much emphasis on reliability as on operational performance. And it must make sure the prime contractors can benefit from doing the same thing.

The defense contractors, in return, need to sell their ideas using the only truly meaningful measure of merit, enhanced combat capability. Clearly someone must do an analysis early on in the process to find the optimal combination of performance, supportability, and reliability, given the threat we face. And since military babies are conceived by contractors, contractors are the logical ones to do this analysis. Then system and support design could be integrated up front, where sound engineering can have the greatest impact.

When anyone in the defense business thinks about performance, he or she must not think about it in a vacuum – that special place where machines never break, and spares and repair parts never need replacing. The combat environment we face today is anything but a vacuum. It's hostile, it's real, and it's demanding. In fact, it too is a special place where the only true measure of merit is force against force, what our systems can do against the enemy's systems whenever and wherever a conflict might occur.

If our systems can't operate because they're so unreliable that we can't support them, then they can't fight either. And that we cannot allow – not when, without adequate logistics, the best people and most sophisticated, powerful weapons will be fighting on the losing side.

CHAPTER 8

Defense and the Military-Industrial Complex

Americans are great ones for casting blame when things go wrong — even when things aren't really all that wrong, and even when the blame is substantially unjustified. When our favorite baseball team loses a game, we blame the nearsighted umpire, the lousy field conditions, or the poor lighting in the stadium. When our children don't do well in school, we blame the teachers, their books, or the local school board. We often fail to acknowledge the real causes — perhaps that our team isn't all that good or that our children aren't studying all that hard.

We also have the unfortunate tendency to attack the very foundations of the life and happiness we enjoy, often without rational or well-defined reasons. For example, some people strike out blindly at all chemicals, feeling that these substances are unnatural and that they threaten physical well-being. Of course, what some people don't realize is that we're all made up of chemicals — various hydrocarbons, amino acids, and enzymes — and that life itself is not only built around chemical reactions, but is, in many ways, enhanced by them. Without the chemistry of modern medicine — the antibiotics, antihistamines, and steroids — our life expectancy might be half what it is today.

In the same way, some people in this country attack other foundations on which American society is built — and from which it gains great sustenance. They cast blame where it is not warranted and in so doing undermine the things that help to secure the blessings of liberty. In effect, they become so obsessed with what they think is dirty bath water and the effect it could have on the baby that they wind up throwing out the bath water and the baby along with it.

Theodore Roosevelt once said that the "only one quality worse than hardness of heart is softness of head." There's been a growing predisposition toward softness of head, especially among those who are critical, by default, of two of the most essential parts of American democracy: the military and the free enterprise system. When these two are combined into what is often disparagingly called the military-industrial complex, the critics' desire to throw out the baby with the bath water becomes even more intense.

The damage to the military-industrial complex from such criticism has been both serious and extensive — and not just in terms of business opportunities lost. Credibility has been forfeited, support has waned, and as a result our nation's defense capability has been undermined during one of the most uncertain periods in its history.

To some extent, the blame rests squarely on the shoulders of those in the military-industrial complex. What negative images have developed they have allowed to develop. What mistakes have been made they didn't need to make. And what criticisms have been leveled at this vital partnership they didn't do a very good job of answering. The members of the defense establishment have, indeed, made themselves a target of opportunity — one which, although fully able to defend itself, has proven substantially inept at doing so.

The kinds of image problems we're talking about here are not new. Such problems actually began two and a half decades ago when the phrase *military-industrial complex* was coined by President Dwight D. Eisenhower during his farewell address to the nation. Eisenhower talked about the need for a dedicated armaments industry. He believed the country could no longer risk "emergency improvisation of national defense, [where] American makers of plowshares could, with time, and as required, make swords as well."

As Eisenhower pointed out then, military realities were evolving into something that bore little relation to those of the past.

Although the kind of large military-industrial complex that he envisioned would, by its very nature, pose certain dangers to our democracy, he felt we could guard against these dangers by having a knowledgeable citizenry and by ensuring the proper coordination of military and industrial activities. He did not argue against having a military-industrial complex, as some would have us believe. He argued only that we would have to devise new mechanisms for dealing with it.

Since then we have not maintained the kind of citizen understanding Eisenhower had hoped for, and the coordination of military and industrial activities has become less and less effective. The result has been a military-industrial partnership under siege in our own society, a partnership attacked more and more frequently often not so much for what it is, but rather, for the harsh realities it symbolizes. The ultimate irony is that Eisenhower's own words have been used time and again out of context, especially by those who oppose either the defense establishment or big business.

It's come to the point today where the words *military-industrial complex* are so laced with emotionalism that most people in the military or private industry avoid using them at all costs. A degrading mythology has developed around our defense industry, a mythology that runs exactly counter to what it should be, given its outstanding performance during and after World War II. If the military and private industry had not worked closely together in a free enterprise environment, much of the technological excellence we've relied on for our survival simply would not exist – and without much doubt, neither would we.

The Arsenal of Democracy

In 1939, when the great threat of Axis tyranny grew relentlessly around us, Franklin Roosevelt recognized the tremendous advantage we had in our free enterprise system. He knew what could be achieved if only private industry had the proper incentives. That's why he dubbed American industry the "Arsenal of Democracy" – and that's why he provided the necessary incentives.

As early as 1938 at the time of the Munich Crisis when Great Britain's Chamberlain government tried to appease Hitler, FDR quietly ordered the armed forces to modernize their wartime production plan. In the spring of 1940, a full 18 months before the Japanese attack on Pearl Harbor, the government began gearing up industry for wartime production. On May 14, 1940, just five weeks before the fall of France, Congress authorized a build up of 4500 military planes. On the next day, as an afterthought, it raised the total to 10,000 aircraft. Industry responded to these challenges with the best equipment in the world in the greatest numbers and at competitive prices.

All those popular myths about a sleepy defense establishment caught off guard by the Japanese attack ignore these careful preparations — and the economic incentives that went hand-in-hand with them. They ignore that, by August 1940, shipyards had already hired 80,000 new workers, and aircraft plants employed an additional 50,000. As huge industrial plants mushroomed overnight, our free enterprise system shook off the last vestiges of the Great Depression and began to show the world just what it was capable of doing.

In 1939, two years before we entered World War II, American factories had already delivered about 3600 military airplanes. But in 1941, it increased production over 500 percent, delivering over 18,000 military airplanes. During 1942, after Pearl Harbor had been attacked and private industry was given the green light to defend democracy, production increased to 47,000 airplanes. The following year, we put another 85,000 warplanes into Allied hands. And in 1944 alone, American free enterprise cranked out another 100,000. The millions of weapons and spare parts we produced during the 44 month period prior to the end of the war allowed us to win that great conflict and prevented the enslavement of the free world. The massive power of our defense industry crushed the forces of tyranny.

We may owe an even greater debt to our free enterprise system for its achievements during the postwar period. During World War II, the towns and cities in America's heartland had been invulnerable. But as modern military technology evolved, our potential adversaries, especially the Soviet Union, developed strategic systems against which there was no defense. We were faced with building a strong and reliable deterrent that could prevent an attack against our country and much of the free world. Considering the speed at which technology was evolving and the ever-growing threat posed by the Soviet Union, this was an undertaking of immense proportions. But even in peacetime during the height of the Cold War years, our free-enterprise system proved capable of producing the required tens of thousands of heavy bombers, transports, fighters, and missiles.

These years constituted a remarkable period for the military, our private defense industry, and this country, because they saw the foundation laid for what has proven to be the most effective deterrent ever known. That period of achievement showed again, to friend and foe alike, what American free enterprise is capable of doing — and above all else, it prevented another world war.

The Soviet Union's Arsenal Approach

Many countries do not rely on free enterprise to provide for their defense. Many rely on a true arsenal system in which the government owns the defense industry and controls the entire weapons production process. In places like the Soviet Union, the production of military materiel is a coherent, fully-funded process under the absolute control of a central military authority.

The Soviets view their defense industry as an integral part of their military capability. And they treat it as such, tightly integrating their industrial base with national defense strategy. That's why the Soviets place their basic defense industrial capabilities under the control of military ministries. Industries producing weapons, such as ICBMs, nuclear warheads, bombers and submarines are integrated with producers of strategic materials such as titanium, aluminum, and beryllium.

For example, the Soviet Defense Ministry of Aviation Industry runs the metal fabrication plants in conjunction with the aluminum industry. These plants, which are designed to produce components for aerospace industries, are located next to final assembly plants. These final assembly plants have excess capacities and employ forging and fabricating technologies that are among the best in the world. The possibilities for boosting production for support of wartime weapons requirements are obvious.

The primary effect of this approach is a far more efficient weapons producing system – one that the military can plan to rely on with great confidence in time of war. The efficiency of the system is evidenced by the impressive growth we've seen in their arsenal capability over the last 35 years and a proven ability to turn out large quantities of weapons quickly.

But what about the negative aspects of using a true arsenal system? The price one would normally pay for this kind of approach is the loss of innovation. The Soviet's arsenal, while disciplined, is also constrained: it tends to reject the kinds of radically new ideas which technological breakthroughs are made of. That's why the Soviet system, often praised for its ability to produce large quantities, has often been criticized for the inferior quality of the weapons it produces.

But that criticism is becoming less and less valid, and our position is becoming more and more tenuous. The Soviets have found several effective ways around this natural limitation. For one thing, they've put a great deal of emphasis on improving their critical defense industries, designating sectors within each basic industry to develop state-of-the-art materials for advanced weapons technology. These concerns now enjoy a very high priority in terms of scarce resources like scientists, equipment, and research.

Additionally, the Soviets have shown an increasing willingness to risk pushing the outer limits of high technology. For example, several years ago they dedicated themselves to developing a high-risk industry for the manufacture of large-scale military equipment using titanium. Today, their technology for processing and fabricating thick plate titanium is at least 10 years ahead of that in the United States. The Soviets have used this capability to construct the fastest and deepest diving attack submarine that exists anywhere, the ALFA.

Another Soviet advantage, which helps to offset the shortcomings of the arsenal approach, is the USSR's vast natural resources. The Soviet Union is the only major industrial nation that is self-sufficient not only in strategic materials but also in energy. It is the world's foremost producer of petroleum and has the largest proven oil reserves outside the Persian Gulf. As an oil exporter, the Soviet Union is second only to Saudi Arabia. And its natural gas reserves and exports are by far the largest in the world.

Finally, and ironically, the Soviets' arsenal system works so well today because they take full advantage of our innovative genius. Simply put, what they can't do themselves, they buy, steal, or collect through open technology transfer. In many cases, they have cashed in on the technology for which we've paid the price — in time and money — to develop.

The Soviets have two major programs for acquiring Western technology. First, a program administered by the Military Industrial Commission of the Presidium of the Council of Ministers is specifically designed to raise the technical sophistication of Soviet weapons. This program seeks one-of-a-kind military and dual-use hardware, blueprints, product samples, and test equipment mainly through espionage, overt collection, scientific exchange programs, and illegal trade. A second program, administered through the Soviet Ministry of Foreign Trade and Soviet intelligence services, seeks to acquire export-controlled microelectronics, computer, communications, machining, robotics, diagnostic, and other equipment to improve Soviet weapons production.

These programs have been very successful. During the early '80s, the first program benefited on the average more than 5000 Soviet military equipment and research programs using Western hardware and technical documents. In the areas of armor, electro-optics, and aviation alone, acquired Western technology saved the Soviets over 100,000 man-years of scientific research. And Western ideas have been directly responsible for hundreds of Soviet military research projects that had not been under consideration, for raising the technical levels of 66 percent of these projects, and for eliminating or shortening phases of more than a thousand military research projects each year.

Thus, the Soviets enjoy, to some extent, the best of both worlds: the coherence and control of a true arsenal system and the innovation that can only come from free enterprise. Figures 9, 10, and 11 document the results of combining a tightly integrated

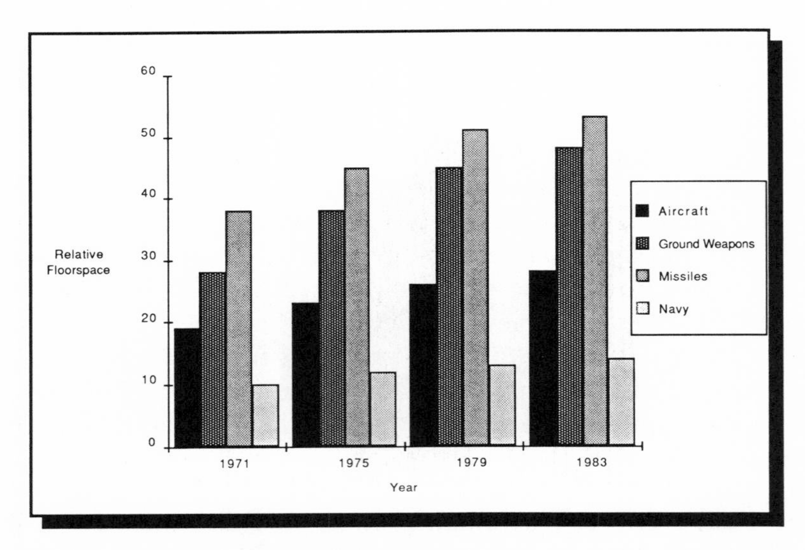

Fig. 9. Soviet Military Production Facilities Floorspace Growth. *(Data from* Soviet Military Power*, 3d ed., Washington, D.C.: U.S. Government Printing Office, April 1984, p. 91.)*

arsenal system with a commitment to defense development possessing ample natural resources and having the willingness and capability to buy or steal Western achievements. The threat is very real.

In Defense of our Defense Industry

What do we have to compete with the efficient Soviet system? We have a defense industrial base withered from years of neglect, critically short of skilled people, suffering from old age, and inhibited by constant streams of criticism. And we have a system of funding and control that is neither coherent nor consistent, and bureaucratic regulations that are both ineffective and burdensome. The result has been declining productivity growth in an industry where productivity growth equates directly to national security.

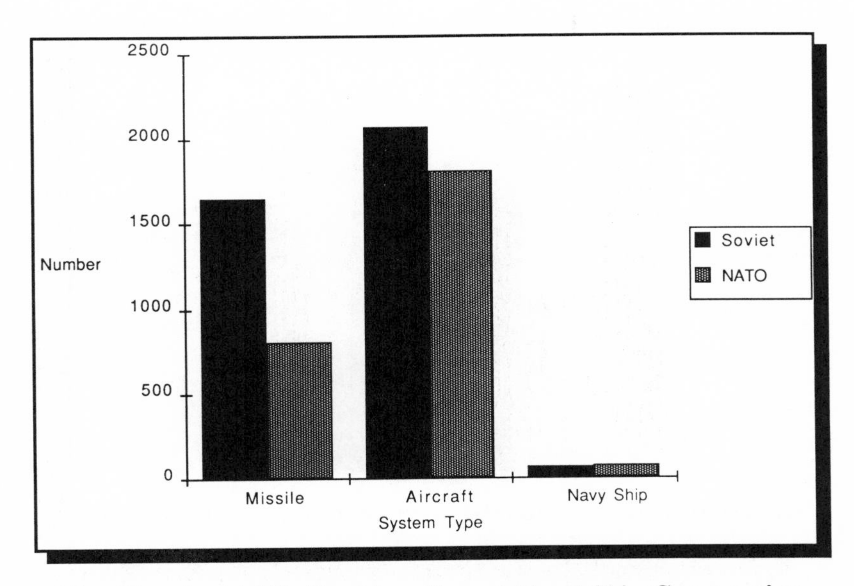

Fig. 10. Soviet Missile, Aircraft, and Naval Ship Construction. *(Data from* Soviet Military Power, *4th ed., Washington, D.C.: U.S. Government Printing Office, April 1985, pp. 38, 87, 105.)*

Today, we have perhaps as many as 30,000 private sector defense and general contractors throughout the United States doing business with the Department of Defense. But the government itself owns only 72 defense production plants, and 14 of these are in stand-by status for emergency use. Since 1965, only one government-owned plant has been built.

Clearly, then, we've put our eggs in the free-enterprise basket. Yet, just as the need for a strong defense system is becoming more critical, criticism of that system is becoming more strident. Why is it so frequently maligned, often by the very people it has benefited the most? Specifically, it suffers because the public does not have a good understanding of defense spending – particularly in terms of the size of military budgets, the impact of this spending on society in general, and the credibility gap created by celebrated cases of defense industry fraud or abuse.

In general, of course, the defense industry shares in the

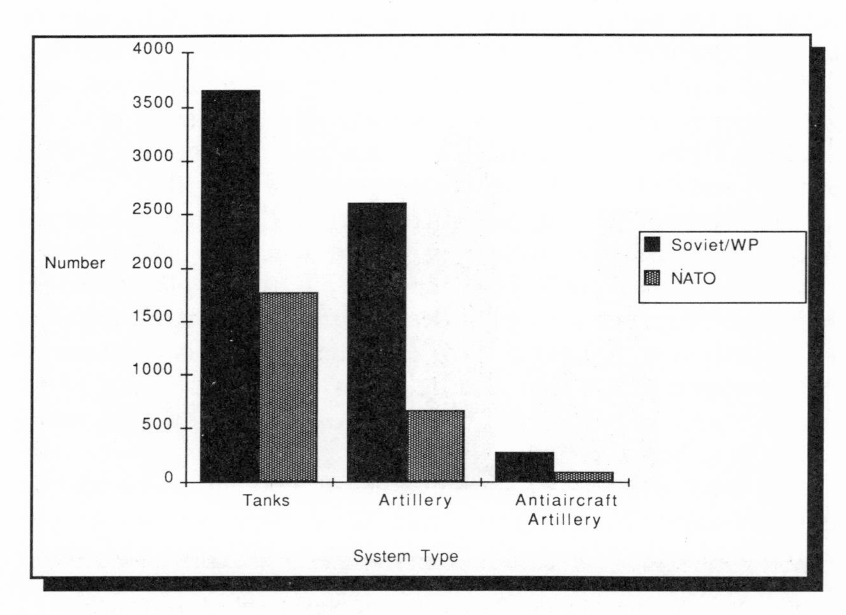

Fig. 11. Soviet/Warsaw Pact *vs* NATO Production of Ground-Forces Materiel.
(Data from Soviet Military Power, *4th ed., Washington, D.C.: U.S. Government Printing Office, April 1985, p. 75.)*

ridicule most big business has been held up to in recent years. Many Americans do not view big business as a positive influence in society. But that's often because they've been taken in by the fictional villainy of, say, J. R. Ewing on TV's *Dallas,* and don't recognize it for the melodrama it really is. The nonprofit Media Institute points out that, "Two out of three businessmen on television are portrayed as foolish, greedy or criminal; almost half of all work activities performed by businessmen involve illegal acts; and television almost never portrays business as a socially useful or economically productive activity."

Certainly some business activities are not productive. But that can be said of any activity in any society at just about any time. In our society today, it is American business that pays the bills and serves as the pump to keep our economy going. One way or another, business pays the salaries most Americans live on, business supplies the fuel which our government runs on, and business provides the essential goods and services that all of us depend on. Indeed, as American business goes, so goes the United States – and to a certain extent, the entire free world.

The defense industry has suffered from the same undeserved image that American business in general has, only perhaps even worse. The size of our defense industry and the large numbers of dollars involved attract a great deal of attention. There's certainly no doubt in anyone's mind these days that defense is big business in this country. But that doesn't mean defense spending is the wasteful and unproductive drain on our economy that many believe it to be.

In 1983, when it was fashionable in many circles to criticize defense budgets for being too large, the dollars spent on defense represented only 17 percent of our total public spending, down from a postwar high of 36 percent in 1955. In fact, defense spending represented only about 6 percent of our gross national product in 1983, less than half of what the Soviets were spending, and about 17 percent of what we spent at the height of World War II.

Of course, the real standard of comparison for defense spending is what not spending on defense would cost us – and not just in terms of life, property, and freedom – but in terms of dollars as well. For example, if we fail to maintain an adequate deterrent and are drawn into, say, another large-scale conventional war, the cost would be astronomical. Just look at what the bill would be to fight World War II again, which was a conventional war until nuclear weapons were used at Hiroshima and Nagasaki. That conflict cost us about $542 billion, including $54 billion that we're still paying for veterans benefits and $200 billion for interest on war loans.

If we took the total price of fighting World War II and assumed just a five percent annual inflation rate since 1945, we'd find that the cost of fighting that war again would exceed 4 trillion dollars – which is considerably more than our entire gross national product. If we took out a 30-year, $4-trillion loan at, say, 12 percent, our payments would exceed $41 billion per month. Thus, assuming we survived the war, we'd be forced to pay around $492 billion annually on our war debt, in addition to whatever the cost of national defense would be then.

That kind of spending could destroy our economy — and with it, our society. So it seems safe to say that fighting a conventional war is not an acceptable alternative, as some contend, to maintaining an adequate nuclear and conventional deterrent. Clearly it is less costly to do what is necessary to prevent a war in the first place than to try to fight one and win.

But defense dollars are not just investments in defense. Money in the military budget is not poured into some dark abyss, never to be seen again. About 41 percent of the '85 defense budget went directly to paying the personnel costs, including salaries, of over 5 million employees in our nation's defense program. And what did they do with the money? They spent it in stores and saved it in banks, credit unions, and savings and loans. They used it to buy cars and homes, to send their kids to school, to pay their taxes, and they gave it to charity. A large part of every defense dollar directly supported hundreds of local communities, many which otherwise would have limited sources of reliable financial support.

A good portion of defense spending also went directly into taxpayers' pockets by creating other jobs and paying other salaries in the private sector. A government defense contract did not just represent money allocated to hardware — it represented productive employment for hundreds of thousands of Americans.

And how about the money put solely into military hardware? Much of it bought the same products the average American consumer buys — from clothes and food to cars and typewriters. Just think about the extent to which American industry directly benefits from military purchases. And think about the share of manufacturing and marketing overhead that the military pays, which otherwise would be passed along to the American consumer in the form of higher prices.

Military spending also provides this nation with another major benefit: technical innovation and scientific discovery. Military applications require a great deal of advanced research in fields ranging from aerodynamics to human factors. Many spin-off technologies, from high speed microprocessors to satellite-based communication systems, benefit the American public in one way or another.

The military-industrial complex also plays a role in educating Americans. How many colleges and universities underwrite their rising costs with defense contracts, industry grants, and ROTC programs — and how many bright students owe their educational opportunities to the defense dollars we've spent? Furthermore, virtually everyone entering the armed forces receives some type of specialty training, whether they become, among other things, truck or aircraft mechanics, computer programmers, or medical technicians. Over the years, their specialized training has contributed a great deal to the well-being of this country.

Most importantly, of course, Americans have received the greatest benefit of all from the investment in defense they've made — after all, we haven't been attacked, and we're still a free and democratic society. But a strong American defense also lends a great deal of credibility to our country and the free world. It creates a stable environment — one in which more business investment may occur. And it gives great underlying strength to the American economy.

Clearly, taxpayers' dollars are not wasted when invested in the nation's defense. Our defense industry is not a dark abyss into which everything good is poured and from which nothing good is returned. But tragically and dangerously, many in this country think it is an abyss, and that's where the members of the military-industrial complex come in.

To start with, it is their job, as members of the defense community, to tell it like it is. In many cases, they have a responsibility to come out of the shadows and put the facts on the table where they can be legitimately and objectively evaluated. Timidity in this regard has served and will continue to serve no cause but the wrong cause. Indeed, in many cases, those in the defense business have been their own worst enemy — they have, at times, sought to stifle the flow of information, to shrink from public questioning instead of making the very sound case for the Arsenal of Democracy. By staying in the shadows, they have contributed to the lack of public understanding and have helped those who seek, for whatever reason, to inhibit the defense effort.

In addition, those responsible for our defense have not always made the best decisions or taken the most prudent actions. Of course, given the size of the defense industry, the complexity of its business, and the dynamic changes in the social, political, economic, and military environments, some problems are likely to occur. But the military and the defense industry can't afford to let such problems develop unattended. They must make that extra effort to never give even the appearance of wastefulness or impropriety. Prudence and honesty in both style and substance will go a long way toward assuring the taxpayers that they're receiving every ounce of national defense possible from every dollar spent. And it will help open their minds to the truly beneficial aspects of a defense partnership where neither partner can survive without the other.

The Problem with Business as Usual

The Yankee ingenuity and drive that gives us our greatest edge is certainly worth preserving. But we're not going to make the most of our innovation and drive if we continue to treat our defense industrial base as business-as-usual in America. The way we're doing things today is not working and will not work in time of war — because, despite all the good ideas we still generate, we no longer have the industrial wherewithal to cash in on them. To the extent we lack the ability to produce weapons, our nation's security is compromised. Thus, we must nurture our defense industry.

The question, of course, is how? Independent and autonomous management, a primary focus on profit, and the opportunity to succeed or fail — these things have always made our economy strong. But free enterprise, constrained as it is by the uncertainties of military requirements and federal spending, is less and less able to perform efficiently in meeting defense needs. New efforts to balance the budget, such as the Gramm-Rudman Bill passed in late 1985, are likely to make matters worse, whereas the reverse should be true. Cuts in the defense budget make it even more imperative that we capitalize on the inherent efficiency of the free-enterprise system in satisfying defense requirements.

To rebuild a defense industry that can meet future challenges, the military must return to the basics of free enterprise and at the same time take into account the unique demands that go with being a partner in the nation's defense establishment. The question, of course, is how the military can avail itself of the undeniable benefits of free enterprise, which is essentially unregulated, and at the same time ensure the American taxpayer (the customer) gets the best possible return on investment in terms of national defense.

The answer is twofold. First, enable the defense industry to truly compete for defense business. That can be achieved only by doing away with the present government cost-accounting procurement system in favor of a pricing approach generally used in private enterprise. Second, recognize that the partnership between the military and the defense industry, like any true partnership, is also built around mutual goals and objectives. Each member of the partnership undertakes separate activities that, when combined, allow both to achieve a goal. In this case, of course, the goal is to remain a secure, free, and democratic society.

Unfortunately, both members of the military-industrial complex no longer seem to view their activities in terms of the overall goal, and neither seems to have a good idea of what the other member is doing. Although the overall goal is national security, for individual corporations, the goal is also to fill a set of contract provisions and at the same time make a profit.

Given these divergent goals, it should come as no surprise that the military and private industry have themselves begun to slug it out in what is fast becoming an adversarial relationship. But we just don't have those kinds of resources to waste any longer. The military must champion the right of private industry to make a fair profit, for profit contributes to our country's health and well-being and forms the basis of our security. But private industry must also honor its obligation to provide a crucial national service.

If the military and the defense industry can't abandon their adversarial relationship, they will play into the hands of those who have called for a dissolution of the partnership. The adversarial approach is not the answer. We don't need to further divorce the military from private industry. In fact, the best solution is just the opposite, to better integrate the military and defense industry — to take better advantage of the strengths shown by this vital partnership.

Our greatest defense resource is free-enterprise innovation. Contractors, not the military, have the talent and experience to produce the best weapons. But they must commit themselves to more than making a profit or fulfilling a contract — they must provide for the national defense. And the military must let contractors know what the defense requirement is, not just the contract requirement — and give contractors an incentive to work the big picture, not just a small piece of it.

A Partnership for Defense

A partnership focused on the common goal of national defense and built around a joint knowledge and understanding of the military's needs would give the military greater access to the contractors' total capability. Instead of the military giving contractors the standard solution, and encouraging them to implement it in the traditional way, the military would describe the overall defense problem and let contractors be more responsible for finding the best solution. This would be a truly integrated system.

For an example of an integrated system, consider the repair process as it's handled by the Air Force today. An AFLC Air Logistics Center benefits from a close integration of various managers, including (1) those overseeing the production of parts, (2) those responsible for the particular weapon systems these parts will be used in, (3) those running the supply and distribution system for these parts, and (4) those in higher command headquarters who plan, monitor, and control the whole operation. The point is that planners and managers know exactly what is happening at any time and are able to maintain control over critical military assets.

When the repair process is contracted out, however, the Air Force effectively trades in this highly integrated system for a set of contract provisions. All the contractor can monitor here are the contract provisions, not the health of the weapon systems themselves. Nor does the contractor have any real sense of the relative importance of the work being done. Consequently, the contractor is unable to adjust its efforts to optimize output — especially in terms of what is really important to the customer, the Air Force.

The repair process, of course, is just a subset of the much larger process of buying new weapon systems, and that process is where the largest gains could be realized from more closely integrating military and industrial activities. We not only spend a great deal of our nation's resources designing and building new weapon systems, but with these designs, we also lock ourselves in for 20 to 30 years of weapon system support costs. In the end, the support costs dwarf the original investment.

As mentioned earlier, contractors effectively determine military requirements in their independent research and development. Through their up-front marketing efforts, they respond to customer needs as they see them. But the needs they're responding to are too narrowly defined. They don't use their genius to work the big problem of, say, providing a system that will ensure air superiority for the European war plan; they work the smaller, more traditionally defined problem of building a fighter to fly so fast, pull so many G's, and have a certain range. There may, in fact, be a far better alternative, one industry hasn't thought of yet because it hasn't really been given either the problem or the opportunity to solve it.

To remedy this shortcoming, we must abandon our present mind-sets and take a cold, hard look at what benefits and dangers would accrue from better integrating our military and private industry (contract) activities. In other words, should the military give senior corporate executives in the defense industry the same information it gives its own generals — that is, the kinds of conflicts being planned for and what capabilities will be required to fight them? These executives would know then, first hand, the requirements for the weapon systems their companies supply and support. They would also have the sensitivity, orientation, and knowledge about defense matters to provide the kind of leadership and management in their organizations that modern military requirements demand.

This approach would not be anything new for our country.

Historically, whenever things have started to fall apart, we've given this kind of access and responsibility to the leaders of private industry. For example, in the opening days of World War II, Franklin Roosevelt created the prototype of an integrated defense partnership, the Advisory Commission on the Council of National Defense. William Knudsen of General Motors, Edward Stettinius of U.S. Steel, Sidney Hillman of the Committee for Industrial Organization, Chester Davis of the Department of Agriculture, and Ralph Budd of the Department of Transportation were the commission's most visible members, and they were given the big defense problems to work on.

Out of the commission came the Office of Production Management, and finally, the War Production Board. The participating captains of industry and labor were told what the country was up against, and they developed the wherewithal for America's armed forces to deal with it. That approach, more than anything else, enabled us to produce fighters like the P-51 and long range bombers like the B-29 – and these weapon systems, more than anything else, allowed us to win World War II.

In the days of the War Production Board, we had time to develop new processes for defense. There's general agreement, however, that we're not likely to enjoy the luxury of time if war comes again. We'll have to fight with whatever partnership arrangement we have, and with whatever skills and materiel we possess at the time. It seems obvious that we need to set up our defense partnership now, while we still have the time.

To do that, we have to do what we did over 40 years ago: give private industry the opportunity to formally pick up the mantle of leadership it properly should carry. It has a legitimate role to play in providing effective, reliable solutions to basic military needs, not just specific weapon system requirements. We should even go so far as to give the defense industry both the incentive and a workable mechanism to challenge military requirements that do not make sense.

These ideas may appear quite radical to some, for they seem to run counter to the normal checks and balances of free-enterprise economics. They create a situation in which the seller has the power to help determine what the buyer needs and in which the buyer is able to influence the seller's activities. But this is not business as usual among *independent* parties. This is a family affair among terribly *interdependent* parties, where failure to achieve the ultimate objective would mean failure for our entire society.

The normal rules of American business don't totally apply here, the same way they often don't apply in any serious, life-and-death situation. There's no doubt that today we face a grave threat, a threat to our way of life and to our very existence. But there's also no doubt that a healthy, innovative, and well-integrated military-industrial complex will help our democracy survive the challenges ahead. We are capable of doing what needs to be done.

The vital partnership of the military and private industry can give us the trump card we need and ensure that we use our limited resources without duplication or waste. But the military must provide American business with the proper incentives, the members of private industry must clearly accept their solemn obligation and responsibility to provide for the national defense, and all members of the military-industrial family must look for new ways to more effectively integrate their activities. Only then will the Arsenal of Democracy continue to live up to its heritage by producing the best material at the lowest price and in the least amount of time.

CHAPTER 9

Managing by the Bottom-Line

For years now, we've not only been denying the growing threat to our democracy, but we've also lacked the military means to meet that threat. The reasons for our denial are many, of course — but perhaps the most significant involves outdated mindsets. We continue to organize and operate a military-industrial complex just as we did in a bygone era. In many ways, we are preparing to fight the last war. Yet, as we've seen in so many ways — from the withering of our defense industrial base to spare-parts overpricing, from excessively long lead times to unreliable systems — the present arrangement is not working.

The solution is to change the way we do things, to better integrate the military and the defense industry so that the entire spectrum of military-industrial activities is focused on the single goal of providing for the national defense. Doing so, of course, represents a gigantic undertaking encompassing a vast set of very difficult problems. They range from the concrete constraints of limited funding to the more abstract impediments of human nature. But the most important step we can take in solving the problem is the first step: determining what we need to do and then devising a coherent system to integrate all the activities of the military-industrial complex to achieve that ultimate goal.

Defining the Goal and the Means of Achieving It

For the military-industrial complex, the ultimate goal is to provide for the nation's security. As Figure 12 shows, the process of meeting that goal begins with a national security policy developed in the political arena. To implement this policy, the Joint Chiefs of Staff draw up various war plans. These plans spell out precisely how to deal with the many possible scenarios in the various regions of the world. For example, there are war plans that provide for a strategic response to a nuclear attack on the United States – and that provide, therefore, our deterrent to global thermonuclear war. Plans also exist for other contingencies in such regions as Europe, East Asia, West Asia, Alaska, and the Western Hemisphere.

The military-industrial complex is responsible for providing the means to successfully carry out these war plans. This role translates into having a force capable of meeting these war plan requirements. To the extent that our present force can meet the war-plan taskings, we have real combat capability; to the extent that it cannot do so, we have deficiencies; and to the extent we have deficiencies, we have requirements for more combat capability.

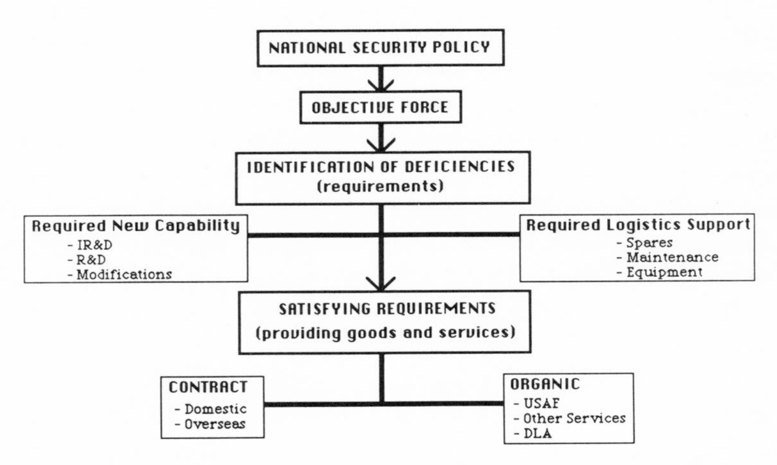

Fig. 12. From National Security Policy to Logistics Support.

An effective management system, then, would first identify the operational capability required by the war plans. To the extent that we need airlift capability, we'd have an airlift requirement, and to the extent that we need air refueling, we'd have an air refueling requirement. In the Air Force alone, there are many such requirements. For example, in the conventional warfare arena, in addition to those already mentioned, there is a requirement to maintain control of the air over the battlefield, a requirement to conduct special missions such as psychological warfare, a requirement to supress enemy defenses and to attack enemy targets on the ground, and there are reconnaissance and command, control, and communications requirements.

Satisfying these requirements means having resources, including trained people and materiel – in effect, goods and services. For the design and production of new systems, we rely almost totally on private industry. And for logistics support (spare parts, engines, repair items, and consumables) we have a similar reliance on the private sector.

If the private sector is to effectively perform its role as a supplier of defense goods and services, it must see how it fits in with the total defense effort. It must become involved in the process, from the war plans on down, so that it can know where the problems lie and where its expertise, experience, and capabilities can most effectively redress deficiencies. In other words, the defense industry must be fully integrated into the military planning process.

Those in private industry can make a tremendous contribution if they're effectively brought into the loop in real time. Because they're the ones who must design and build systems to meet the wartime tasking – and they're the ones who must provide the spare parts and other logistics support necessary for these systems to actually do their assigned operational, war-plan taskings. But to do so effectively, private industry must be constantly in sync with evolving military requirements.

A bottom-line management system called *meaningful measures of merit* is the kind of approach that can help achieve real-time integration. It is designed to ensure that the actions we take and the resources we allocate, both in the military and private sector, contribute to the bottom-line of providing for the nation's security.

Identifying the Meaningful Measure of Merit

We can do that by simply extending the power of common sense with the capability modern technology gives us. By taking better advantage of such things as readily available high-speed data systems, telecommunications, and artificial intelligence, we can now design and implement a system that will identify, evaluate, and then prioritize, in advance, the problems that need to be solved and guide us as to how our scarce resources should be allocated to solve them. Such an approach could be used for almost any set of problems, from making money in business to managing one's personal life.

As pointed out in Chapter 5, even we, as ordinary consumers, must often decide how to allocate resources. Certainly we must allocate our time. Then we must allocate our money, which these days can be the most difficult decision of all. What we are striving to achieve is the best return possible on the investment of our resources. But to realize that objective, we must know two things. First, what type of return are we seeking – that is, what is our objective? And second, how do we measure this objective and the resources needed to achieve it?

Some resource decisions are effectively made for us. For example, the decision on what to do with our time during working hours is usually made by our employers. Granted, there are countless other decisions that must be made while on the job, and these will be addressed later. However, the basic decisions of when and where work is to be accomplished are normally conditions of employment, and hence, literally taken out of our hands. In addition, we must also allocate time for such basic activities as eating and sleeping. The real time-allocation choices we face are in the areas of recreation and entertainment – or those things that round out the quality of our lives.

These choices are usually more difficult for two reasons. First, there's much less restriction on what we choose, making the possibilities significantly greater than what we have in the work environment. And second, virtually any choice we make costs money, and this brings into play the major variable of financial resources. And since, for most of us, money is one of the most limiting resources, we're required to establish priorities, determining in advance the relative importance and affordability of what we want to do in our free time. By the way, time can play a dominating role in our decision. For example, some things, although of lesser importance than others, can only be satisfied at a certain time — like going on a summer vacation or attending a professional football game on Sunday.

The point of this discussion is simply that everyday life is substantially an exercise in resource acquisition and allocation. Anything from eating dinner to buying a car, from attending the opera to taking a shower, requires both time and money. And since both time and money are finite resources, our goals must be clearly defined and prioritized and then reconciled with available resources. There must be some mechanism then for tracking and measuring how well we're doing and making necessary adjustments. That, in a nutshell, is the purpose of the meaningful-measures-of-merits concept for managing resources.

An important aspect of this type of management system is the ability to display data so that the various resources are visually related to the goal at hand. There are, of course, many good ways to do this. Bar and column charts, line and area graphs, and color or pattern coded indicators all can provide effective representations of management data. In this chapter, the vectorgraph, a slightly different display system, will be used. The vectorgraph is basically a pattern-coded line graph of resources. The points on the graph are spread around a central point, which represents the goal. The inner ring is satisfactory, the middle ring is marginal, and the outer ring is unsatisfactory. Each resource is weighted according to its relative importance in achieving this goal. Using this weighting, points for each resource are plotted in the appropriate ring.

Figure 13 shows an admittedly simplistic, but useful, example: vectorgraph charts for managing money in one's personal life. Suppose, in this instance, a family is having problems making ends

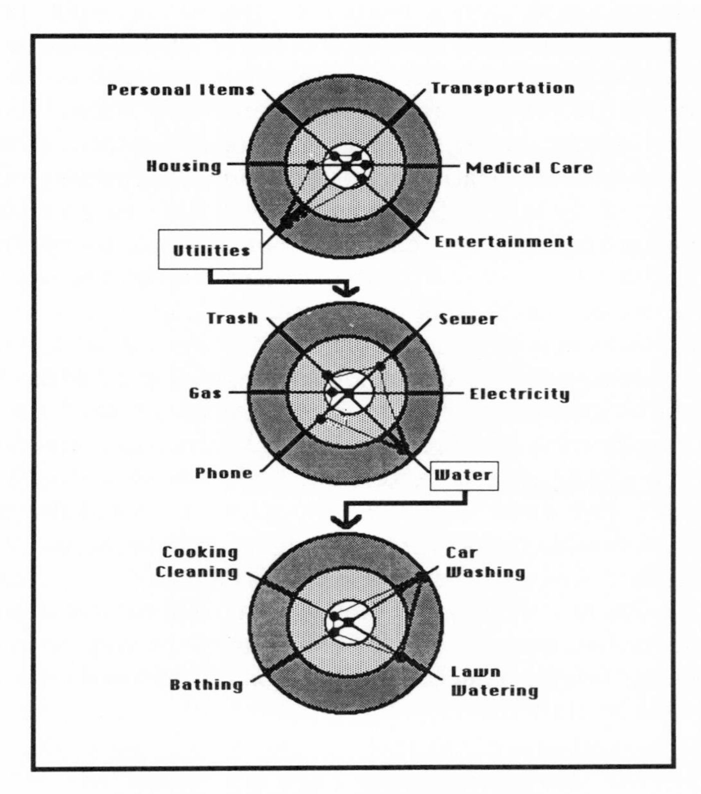

Fig. 13. Vectograph Example.

meet. For them, the goal is to live a good, comfortable life that is more affordable. Where's the problem and what can be done about it? The problem is obvious: they're spending more than they can afford. But what to do about it – that's really the key question here. Of course one solution would be to make more money, but let's suppose that's not an option available to this family. The solution must therefore involve trimming expenses.

The top vectorgraph displays hypothetical data for the family's major expense categories: utilities, housing, personal items, transportation, medical care, and entertainment. Each category has been weighted according to its importance and average costs in the region where they live, so the display actually provides a sense of what balance exists in terms of the resource actions the family can take. For example, even though housing probably represents the single greatest expense, in this case, the dollar outlay is almost in accord with housing costs throughout the region. In addition, the importance of housing is paramount, and the ability of the family to reduce this expense is severely limited by a mortgage and local taxes and insurance. So even though housing may cost a lot, in terms of resource management, the cost is not too far out of line.

But look at utility costs. Given normal expectations, and their contribution to the overall goal, utility costs are too high. Tracking utilities down to the second vectorgraph, it's not hard to see why. Utility costs are being driven up by excessive water usage. Now this isn't to say that water costs more than electricity, because it doesn't. But given water's relative importance and the normal costs one would expect to pay for water, its costs in this case are out of line.

The third vectorgraph provides the information needed to take corrective measures. Given the bottom-line goal of living an *affordable*, comfortable life, perhaps car washing and lawn watering could be cut back.

The Meaningful Measure of Military Merit

Because of the military's size, importance and dynamic nature, managing military resources is an infinitely more complex task than getting a handle on one's personal finances. That's why the military-industrial complex could benefit so much from bottom-line management.

For military operations, the bottom-line (or the objective) is combat capability. To that end, we can design high-tech systems today that will look at the specific requirements of a general requirement along with the variables involved and lay out the status of each of these variables in terms of achieving our goals. In effect, such a system would provide up front a clearly defined set of requirements down through all the levels of the system — and it would identify the meaningful measure of merit for each of the resource expenditures we're pursuing. In the process, it would also tell us early on, while there's still enough time to act, how and where to allocate scarce resources like money and human talent to achieve our objectives.

Allocating scarce resources to provide combat support is one of the most important requirements of national defense today, so we'll look here at a hypothetical application of the meaningful-measures philosophy centering on the logistics process. The first step is to define precisely what the purpose or goal is, because activities and processes are only meaningful to the extent they contribute to this overall purpose or goal. In the case of logistics, the goal is to provide those goods and services necessary to ensure that the weapon systems of the United States armed forces can do their wartime tasking.

The next step is to identify the resource requirements necessary to perform the mission and then identify those resources available. This step is followed by listing the various processes and activities of the organization that actually allocate these resources — and then evaluating their relative contribution to the overall mission.

There are two basic benefits to this approach. First, by looking at the relative contribution of each activity, both military and industry executives can prioritize the allocation of scarce resources in a sound, systematic manner. And second, those involved in each activity can know, in advance, what actions will be necessary to achieve the overall purpose or goal. The point is to determine resource needs well in advance so as not to be caught lead-time away from doing something that has to be done now, simply because we lacked the visibility to know that these particular resources would be needed.

Managing by War-Plan Requirements

Military merit is the ability to execute war plans — and that requires combat capability. For any particular war plan, combat capability can be further broken down into needed operational capabilities (strategic airlift, air refueling, and so on). These capabilities, in turn, can be defined in terms of required weapon systems (long-range transports to provide strategic airlift, aerial tankers to provide air-to-air refueling, and so on), along with their required utilization rates.

Our management system would begin, then, by determining what is required in each war plan for each weapon system and the relative importance each weapon system has to the success of that plan. And it would consider real world status and possible changes during the planning, assessment, and execution phases. This approach provides a way to determine the need and priority of each weapon system to be supported. And this, in turn, creates the basis of determining, in real time, the relative priority of the logistics requirements — and ensuring, preferably in advance, that these requirements can be met.

For example, consider a typical war-plan scenario for the F-15 fighter. That plane is our first-line air superiority fighter, the one we rely on to give us control of the skies. The success of the whole plan thus depends on that single system. Unless we can clear the skies of enemy fighters, there can be no reliable airlift, and without reliable airlift — and the personnel, materiel, and supplies it provides — we would lose the war. It's just that simple.

The defense industry has a great responsibility here. It must design and build weapon systems, including the F-15, not just to meet contract specifications developed around what was traditionally done in the past. It must also provide a system that gives the military the kind of superiority that a wartime environment will demand. A good start in doing just that is to design and build weapon systems like the F-15 that are so reliable they can be deployed without logistics support.

Of course, that hasn't been done yet. All of our weapon systems today, including the F-15, demand a great deal of logistics support. The important point here is that the military and defense industry can't manage logistics support for critical, complex systems like the F-15 in a vacuum. It has to be managed in terms of the bigger picture. No single element of logistics support can be viewed as an end in itself but rather should be viewed in terms of the contribution it makes to the overall mission.

Let's return to the typical war plan. The vectorgraph display in Figure 14 shows the Air Force's operational requirements, or designed operational capabilities (DOCs). Each vector radiating out from the center indicates the relative supportability of each DOC in the war plan with a weighted scale running from 100 percent supportable in the center to totally unsupportable at the outside perimeter. A DOC that is 80 to 100 percent supportable is plotted in the center, or satisfactory area; one that is 60 to 79 percent supportable is plotted in the middle, or marginal ring area; and one that is less than 60 percent supportable is plotted in the outer, or unsatisfactory ring.

Now let's suppose that strategic airlift is rated at 65 percent supportable, or marginal, as indicated in Figure 14. Given the importance of airlift to the success of the entire war plan, this rating would mean that the entire war plan is only marginally supportable. Thus, bringing this particular measure back to a satisfactory rating would be a top priority.

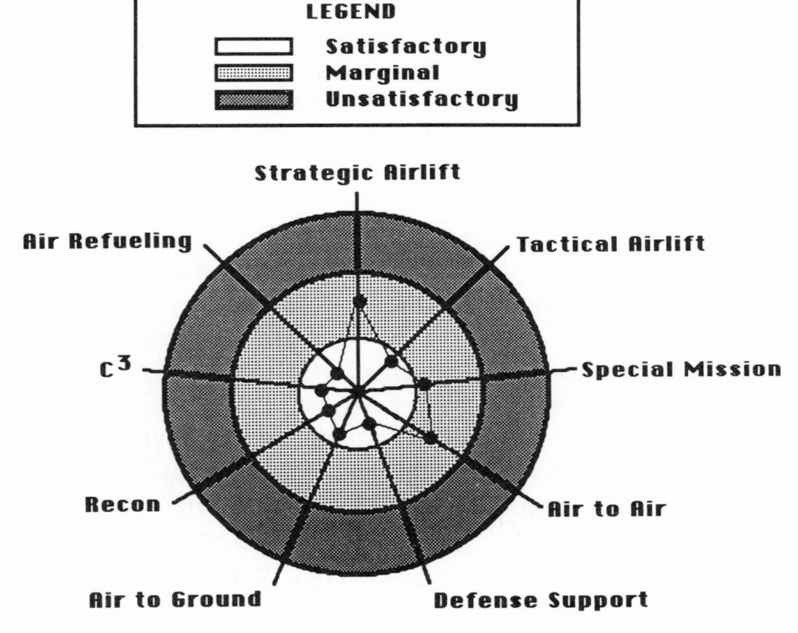

Fig. 14. Displaying War Plan Designed Operational Capabilities (DOC).

To do that, we have to know precisely why airlift is rated as marginal. We need to drop down one level and look at strategic airlift systems themselves. As you can see in Figure 15, this simulated problem centers on the C-5 and C-141 (which together make up our strategic airlift capability). The C-141 has a satisfactory rating, but the C-5, which provides our only outsized-load airlift capability, is dangerously unsupportable.

Figure 16 shows the indicators of supportability in time of war for the C-5 transport aircraft. Of course, a certain number of C-5 resources are already in the system, providing for peacetime operations. These resources include, in addition to the aircraft themselves, the spare parts, spare engines, and support equipment necessary to fly them. In effect, these so called peacetime resources constitute our readiness to begin fighting. But in a typical wartime scenario, we'll have to be ready to sustain our efforts. When the conflict begins, we must be able to quickly increase, or surge our support, to meet a rapidly intensifying situation. Our ability to do this is called *initial sustainability*. Then, after this initial surge,

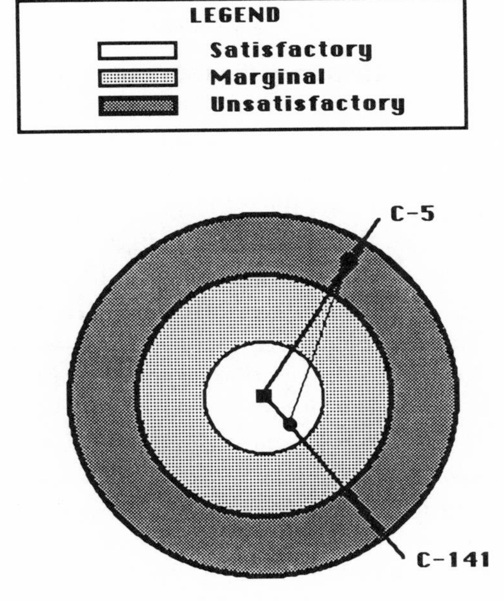

Fig. 15. Tracking Airlift Capabilities in Terms of War-Plan Tasking.

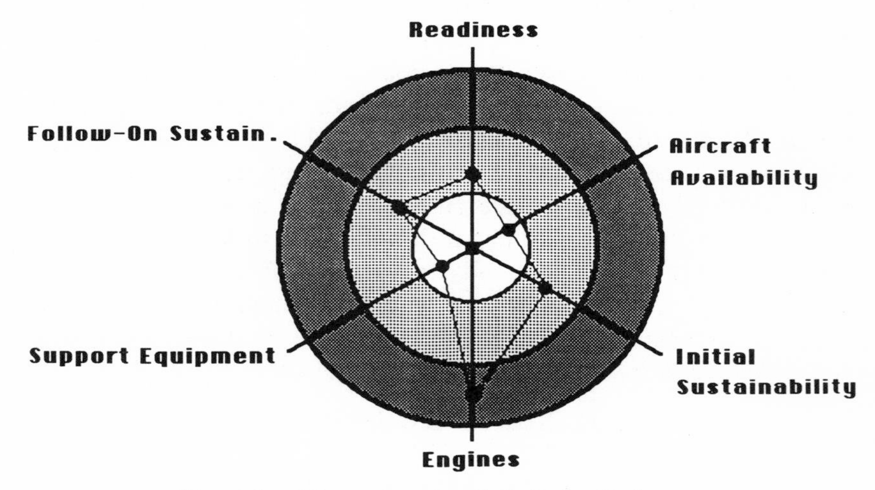

Fig. 16. Measuring the C-5s Pulse Points.

we must provide a stable level of support until the conflict can be resolved favorably. This is called *follow-on sustainability*.

Information, like that provided in Figure 16, would give all the prime decision makers involved with the C-5 (in this case, military leaders and executives from such corporations as Lockheed and General Electric) a picture of the resources required to do the job. And since the relative importance of these resources would have already been weighted by the contribution made to the mission, they'd have the means now of comparing, in a meaningful way, the system's supportability in terms of war-plan tasking. If they had information like that plotted in Figure 16, they could determine where the problem lies and where the priority in allocating resources must be placed. In this example, the most serious C-5 deficiencies are indicated in engine support.

Figure 17, which zooms in on C-5 engine measures, further defines the problem area. The major concern is clearly a lack of serviceable engines, in part because of supply shortfalls but primarily because of whole-up engine stock level deficiencies. Thus, to ensure that the war plan could be supported, it would be necessary to increase the number of C-5 engines in stock.

But what, exactly, needs to be done? Figure 18 helps us find the answer, as it takes us one more level into the engine problem. Although transport time (getting engines where they need to be) is satisfactory, and there are plenty of spare engines, two areas of concern stand out. The operating bases aren't capable of repairing engines quickly enough in the event of war, and processing engines through supply depots takes too long.

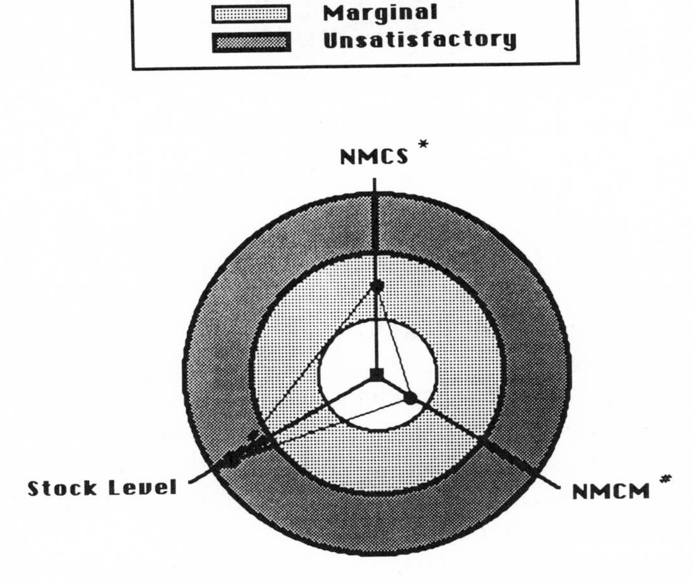

*NMCS - Not Mission Capable / Awaiting Supply
*NMCM - Not Mission Capable / Awaiting Maintenance

Fig. 17. C-5 Engine Measures.

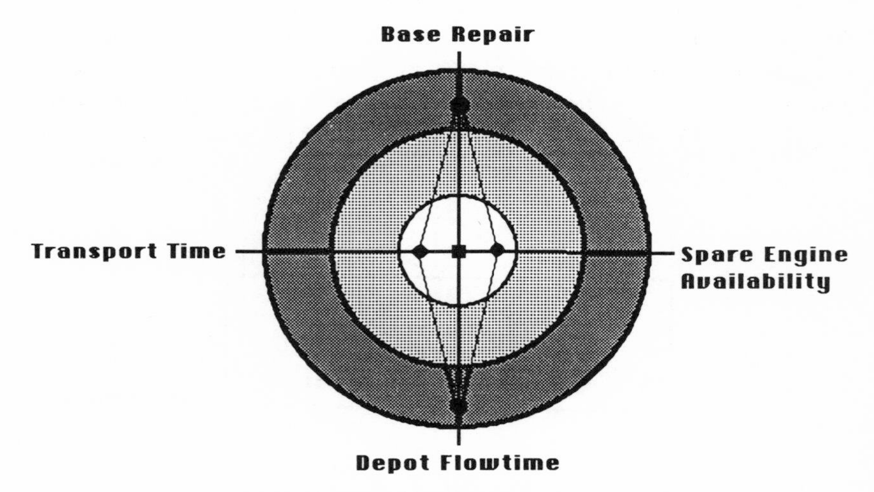

Fig. 18. Discovering the Engine Stock-Level Problem.

Analyzing the Logistics Process

At this point, we need to look at the logistics process itself — at what exactly is causing the problem and how it can be redressed. The purpose is to correlate weapon system supportability to the logistics process. As Figure 19 shows, we would need to assess the main logistics processes of acquisition, distribution, requirements identification, and maintenance, along with quality assurance and base support.

We've already traced DOC deficiencies to airlift, airlift deficiences to the C-5, C-5 deficiencies to engines, engine deficiencies to stock level shortfalls, and finally, stock level shortfalls to base level repair and depot flowtimes.

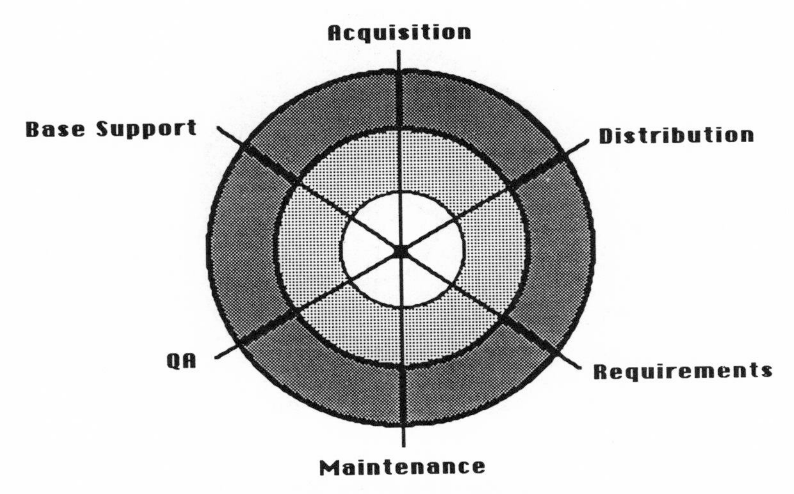

Fig. 19. The Logistics Processes.

Now let's zero in on the maintenance process, and consider the base level repair problem. Base level engine repair involves three kinds of activities, as shown in Figure 20: periodic inspections, unscheduled maintenance, and routines in a test cell (a place where engines can be run and tested under laboratory conditions off the airplane). Let's say that we experienced an abnormally high failure rate of engines being cell tested. Our next step is to drop down another level and look at the test cell measures and find out why.

Typically an engine in a test cell is run, and its inlet temperature, thrust, RPM, fuel flow, and vibration are measured. Suppose, for this hypothetical example, turbine inlet temperatures in several engines were suddenly exceeding the maximum limit, as

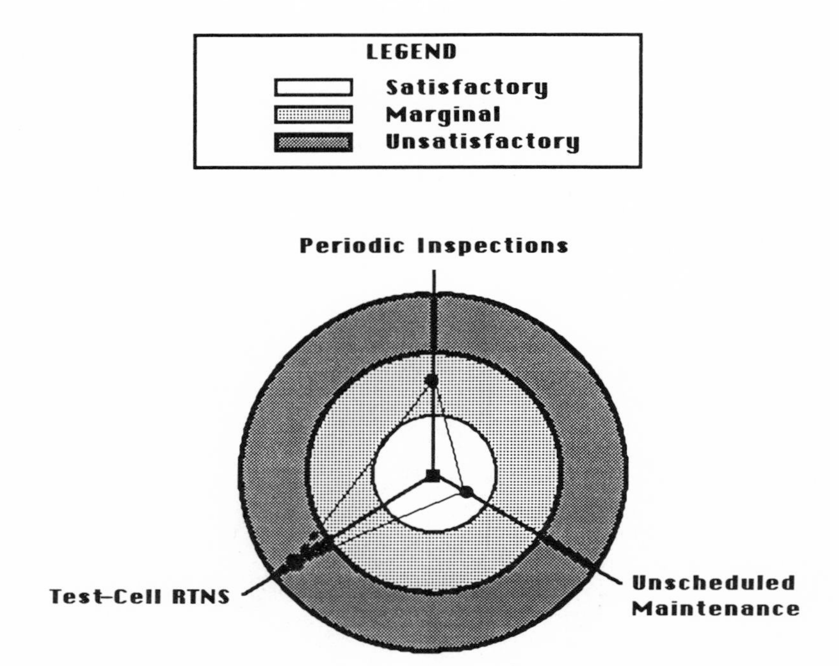

Fig. 20. Base-Level-Support Pulse Points.

indicated in Figure 21. Since this kind of generic problem probably involves either a design defect with the engine or perhaps the test cell itself, the contractor would clearly be the one in the best position to step in and solve it.

And that's the real value – because whatever the problem may be, as long as it exists, it would limit our ability to do the wartime tasking, and to some extent, compromise our national security strategy. The more visibility contractors have over such problems and the better able they are to relate them to the ultimate goal of national security, the faster they can act, and the more secure this nation will be.

The same thing would hold true for the depot flowtime problem. Figure 22 shows the various engine types repaired or modified at San Antonio Air Logistics Center. And as indicated earlier in our wartime assessment, we see a very definite problem with the

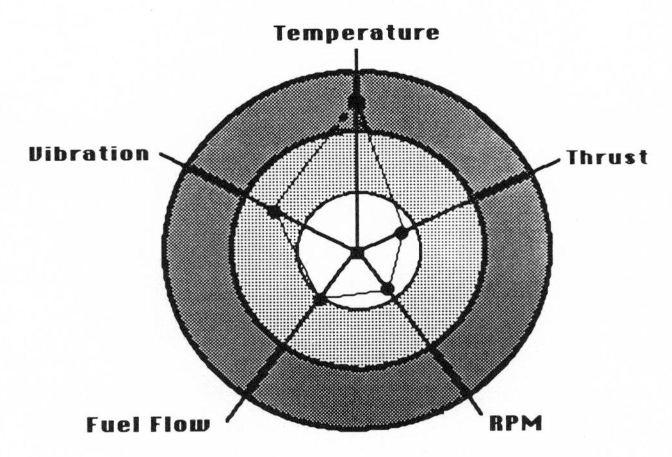

Fig. 21. Test-Cell Pulse Points.

TF39 engine, which powers the C-5 aircraft. But what part of the logistics process is responsible? And what resources can be reallocated to deal with the situation?

Figure 23 measures TF39 engine depot maintenance in terms of data, spare parts, support equipment availability, workmanship, facilities, and manpower. This vectorgraph shows definite shortfalls in manpower. By improving the manpower rating, we could significantly improve the C-5's supportability. And given the importance of this system, we could also significantly improve the supportability of the whole war plan.

But what are the problems contributing to the manpower shortfalls on the C-5 engine line? For the answer, we drop yet another level and analyze manpower. The vectorgraph in Figure 24 shows that the authorization is adequate, there are enough people actually assigned, and turnover is quite reasonable. But the skill

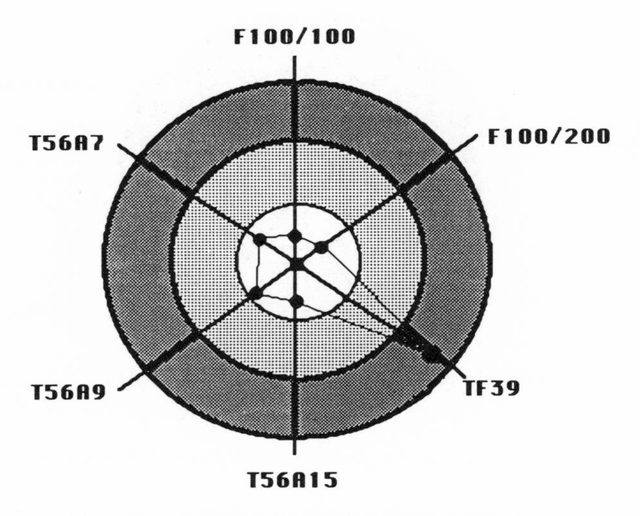

Fig. 22. Depot Flowtime Pulse Points.

levels are too low – indicating, in this hypothetical example, shortfalls in the training area.

The short-term solution to the problem is simple: bolster C-5 engine repair by moving repair personnel with transferable skills from the engine lines of less critical weapon systems. That alone will improve the supportability of the war plan without requiring additional resources.

In addition, we must find ways to improve, over the longer term, the productivity of our C-5 engine technicians. Traditionally, we would look at putting additional resources into improving

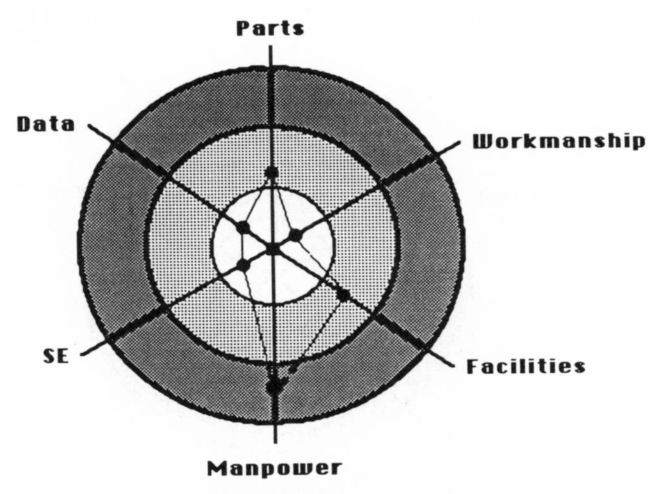

Fig. 23. TF39 Engine-Maintenance Pulse Points.

our training programs and thereby raise the relative skill level of our maintenance people.

But maybe, if contractors could see the same kind of analysis that we have just done, they could come up with another solution – because they would now better understand the problem. Given the importance to our national security of reducing problems with the C-5 aircraft, someone in the private sector would probably seize the opportunity to develop new types of test and maintenance equipment. Equipment that would permit those with lower-level skills to accomplish the same tasks would solve a pressing defense problem and no doubt make the contractor some money in the process.

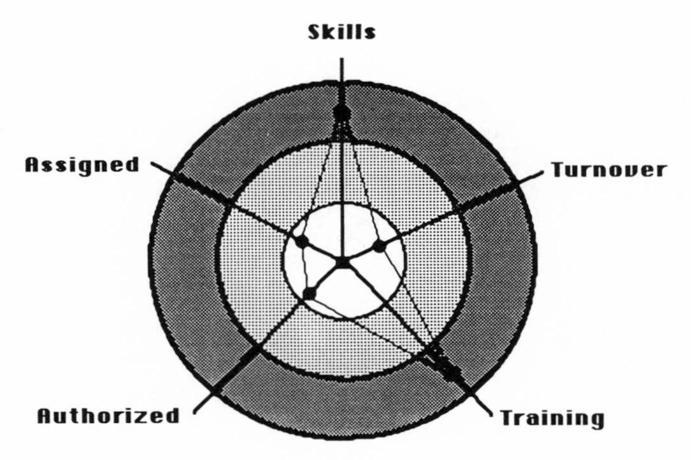

Fig. 24. Manpower Pulse Points.

Drawing Conclusions

It's important, at this point, to remember that we're not talking about *reacting* to a peacetime support problem, we're talking about *preventing* a wartime support problem. The inlet temperature and depot flowtime problems would not, in and of themselves, necessarily impact peacetime flying, because we would probably have enough spare engines to do that. But these problems would really affect us in time of war. By then, if we hadn't already found a solution, our entire defense effort could easily be compromised — because we probably wouldn't have the time necessary to solve them.

One more point about what's been described here: what we've looked at so far are just two hypothetical problem areas of one weapon system of one DOC of one war plan. An effective logistics management system must be able to track through the use of modern data and telecommunication technology all the problem areas of all the weapon systems of all the DOCs of all the major war plans, and it must do so continuously, moment by moment. And ultimately, it must be made available to all the major players in the military-industrial complex.

This approach could effectively integrate the military with private industry and better provide for our national security. As a bottom-line management system, it begins with the mission, the reason the military-industrial complex exists in the first place. Then, through a logical progression, it breaks down challenges into the specific requirements and shows how resources are being matched against these requirements.

Although we have only sampled such a system in a conceptual way, this approach is not merely a concept. It has a track record of having been applied successfully in a number of equally complex resource management environments, the most complex of which is the one from which these illustrations have been created. It works, and it can provide the means for coming to grips with our current overall resource allocation challenge — not only in the Department of Defense and the military-industrial complex, but in all phases of government and business where resource allocations must be made.

Meaningful measures of merit, then, is an effective approach — because it helps guide us in making difficult decisions, and it does so early on, while enough time still remains. It is a way to solve, to the greatest extent possible, problems for which there are no easy solutions. It is a system for managing, in the best way possible, resources that may otherwise be inadequate to do the job. These are the very realities now facing the military-industrial complex, and meaningful measures of merit is the kind of integrated, bottom-line management system needed to deal with these realities.

CHAPTER 10

The Lessons of Louisbourg

Up on Cape Breton Island on Canada's east coast stand the remains of an old fortress named Louisbourg. The story of Louisbourg began in the middle of the 18th century, during what was called King George's War. But the implications of Louisbourg are substantial for us today. Indeed, the story of Louisbourg exemplifies what this book is all about – that there are certain harsh realities of life we must accept, that there are tough decisions that we must make and then live by, and that the consequences of not doing so can be both grave and permanent.

Louisbourg was a French bastion that effectively controlled the entrance to North America. France, at the time, was the greatest world power, but more and more, it was being challenged by a rapidly expanding British empire. During King George's War, Louisbourg had been captured by the British. However, in 1748, to their bitter disappointment, the British had to give it back under a treaty that called for mutual restoration of conquered territory.

But the savagery of man still existed, desire still exceeded the resources available, and that treaty, like so many, led only to a contrived peace. Within eight years, a new war broke out. This war, called The Seven Years' War, is not well-known among U.S. citizens. Yet, it was one of the most important occurrences in our history as a nation. For had that war not occurred, Americans' national tongue might well be French.

But the war did happen, France was destroyed as a world power, England did become the colonizer of the globe, and the stage was set for the American Revolution. And the decisive battle of the Seven Years' War, the one that effectively changed the course of human history, was the Battle of Louisbourg.

By the time of the Seven Years' War, the French had built Louisbourg into the strongest fortress on the American continent. It was strategically located on a tongue of land at the entrance to a land-locked bay overlooking the sea to the east. And it boasted a circuit of fortifications more than a mile and a half long.

The fortress housed a garrison of four battalions, including two companies of artillery and 24 companies of troops – in all, 3080 regular troops, plus officers, armed inhabitants, and even a band of allied indians. And it boasted 219 cannon and 17 mortars mounted on the walls and outworks. The French considered the fortress and the North American continent impregnable.

The British assaulted the fortress on July 16, 1758 – and within a few days, only four cannon were left to defend Louisbourg's front area. On July 26, the last of these cannon was silenced. But what happened? Why did Louisbourg fall? How could the French – with the firepower and manpower and with the experience of losing the Fortress only a few years earlier – let it happen again? They had the strategic location, the provisions, and plenty of warning. What went wrong?

At Louisbourg, there had been a shortage of high quality building materials. But the French didn't use these quality materials to build the walls and outworks – they used them to build the King's storehouses and Governor's Quarters. And when the time came for Louisbourg's guns to fire, the walls gave way under the concussion. Thus, a seemingly minor error in resource allocation affected a relatively isolated event, but the impact on the course of human history turned out to be enormous.

The French could not see the forest for the trees – they had skimped on building military excellence, using their best materials instead to improve the good life. And they wound up making their weapon systems useless and losing the good life altogether. They simply were unable to make the sacrifices necessary to break free of old mind-sets and provide for an adequate defense. They had somehow deceived themselves into thinking they had the necessary military capability. Yet they found out the hard way that their capability was a myth and that myths don't count for much in a war.

The lesson of Louisbourg is clear enough for us today. Like the French in the 1750s, we currently face a serious military threat – and we manage, on a day-to-day basis, an unending series of seemingly minor, isolated events. And any one of these could have a profound impact on our future as a great society and the course of human history.

Yet many Americans today, like the French at Louisbourg, cannot see the forest for the trees. They seem unwilling to sacrifice the good life in order to build an adequate defense. As a nation, we spend almost as much on recreation as we do on defense. We spend more on alcoholic beverages than we do equipping and operating our Air Force. And we spend twice as much on non-durable toys and sports supplies than we do on the Air Force's strategic capability. This is particularly troublesome, since the Air Force has the highest funding of all the Services – almost $4 billion more than the Navy and more than $25 billion more than the Army in the FY 85 budget alone.

Furthermore, those in the military-industrial complex have fallen victim to past mind-sets, preparing to fight the last war by emphasizing operational performance parameters without regard to reliability and supportability. They've ignored the signs that the system isn't working, they've ignored the realities of come-as-you-are warfare, and like the French at Louisbourg, they have not managed their scarce resources according to the bottom-line. The result: the walls could well come tumbling down if they're ever put to the test.

Standing on the mounds that were once the King's Bastion at Louisbourg, one can look out at the glistening sea, reflect on the events of mankind's history, and better understand the dangers our country faces today. Standing there, one can better understand just what our responsibilities, as free citizens, really are in that regard. We must not play down or dismiss the relevance of seemingly isolated events when, as history has shown us, the impact can be enormous. We must not allow what happened to the French in 1758 to ever happen to us – because not only are we the key to a continent, we're the key to democracy and freedom on this planet.

Our means of making sure that doesn't happen is a healthy

military-industrial complex — the only source of real combat capability our society possesses. It's imperative, therefore, that we ensure our cannon are mounted on firm walls — walls built with a strong, viable, and well-integrated defense-industrial base that manages its resources by the bottom-line and that actively campaigns for public support — walls built with strategy, tactics, and logistics that are keyed to the realities of modern warfare — and walls built with the traditional American desire to push at the outer limits of accomplishment, to achieve all of the excellence possible, and to be all that the greatest democracy in the history of mankind can still be.

Index